THE PAST

Learning from what goes wrong

PETER FISHERMAN

DayOne

© Day One Publications 2024

ISBN 978-1-84625-778-0

All Scripture quotations, unless stated otherwise, are from The Holy Bible,
New International Version Copyright © 1973, 1978, 1984 International Bible Society

British Library Cataloguing in Publication Data available

Published by Day One Publications
Ryelands Road, Leominster, HR6 8NZ
Telephone 01568 613 740
Toll Free 888 329 6630 (North America)
email—sales@dayone.co.uk
web site—www.dayone.co.uk

All rights reserved
No part of this publication may be reproduced, or stored in a retrieval system, or transmitted, in any form or by any means, mechanical, electronic, photocopying, recording or otherwise, without the prior permission of Day One Publications.

Printed by 4edge Limited

*'My dear brothers, stand firm. Let nothing move you.
Always give yourselves fully to the work of the Lord,
because you know that your labour in the Lord is not in vain'*
(1 Corinthians 15:58)

4 The Pastorate

Commendations

I must say right at the beginning that I very, very much enjoyed this book!

Murphy's Law—if things can go wrong, they will go wrong! Alas, that 'law' seems to be played out with a vengeance in too many a local church, aided by the variable factors of human nature and our old adversary, the devil.

The wise 'Fisherman' author here, with candour but not contempt, and with honesty, humour, and no sense of hopelessness, introduces us to the 'pool-life' of many congregations. The cold fish, who want to stay that way; the exotic ones who resent any change to the temperature of their particular puddle; the large creatures who take up a lot of space and time; and the occasional sharks whose mission appears to be to bite and devour any who get in their way. And all in the sight of the Great Fisherman Himself, sustaining His sometimes 'weary, worn and sad' trawler skippers, until the final catch is landed.

All in all, a most helpful and delightful read for every 'fisher of men and women'—well-written, insightful, encouraging, practical, wise, and wonderfully quotable! Highly recommended!

Dr Steve Brady
(Steve is the senior pastor at First Baptist Church of Grand Cayman, West Indies. He held four pastorates in the UK before serving for some twenty years as Principal of Moorlands College, which trains people for Christian service in the UK and overseas. He has spoken at conferences and conventions around the world and holds a PhD degree in theology. He is the author, contributor and editor of over twenty books.)

There are myriad books on pastoring. Many are concerned with pastoring in yesterday's churches and there are a variety of books dealing with pastoring in today's churches. Some have been written by the great historical divines, some by modern pastors with varying experience and some by those

Commendations

who have little practical knowledge of the challenges and heartaches of pastoring God's people. They range from expounding scriptural principles to describing autobiographical achievements and successes.

It is therefore refreshingly honest and reassuringly frank to read a book which is not ashamed to address the true character of practical pastoring, warts and all. This book takes the lid off what can sometimes be the mysterious world of the pastor.

Having been engaged in both training and pastoral work for over fifty years, I am heartened by the down-to-earth, up-to-heaven lessons from which everyone in a church may benefit, including, not least, the pastoral leadership itself. From pulpit to pew, vestry to study, chapel door to garden gate, this author embraces the day to day stepping stones and pitfalls of the pastorate. There are timely lessons to be duly learned and crucial warnings to be promptly heeded.

As under-shepherds in the church of Jesus Christ, pastors will feel their ministry extremely daunting at times. But in serving the Chief Pastor, the serving of his flock will be both a demand and a delight. This experienced author has shared his pastoral experiences from mountain-tops to minefields, and in that he provides a valuable insight from which every shepherd and sheep may benefit.

This book is immensely practical and should be read widely by both those in the pew and in the pulpit.

Geoff Fox
(For more than forty years Geoff has been the pastor of Haven Church, Gorran Haven, Cornwall, and has provided vocational theology training to numerous groups of students nationally, including those aspiring to pastoral ministries.)

A very useful book for pastors and their wives.
Philip Grist
(Philip served for many years as a missionary in India with Grace Baptist Mission.)

Commendations

Having been a pastor now for seventeen years, and though the church I pastor has looked after me well during those years, I can't help wishing that this book had been around when I started out in ministry. I haven't experienced all the issues described in the book, but many just like them. I enjoyed the honesty of the author and his willingness to address his own failings in hindsight and to challenge some of the notions that a pastor has to put up with people's thoughtlessness and unkindness without a word.

On a practical level this book would have given me a great place from which to start, not least around negotiating a contract. There is a degree of naivety when it comes to starting your first pastorate, a desire not to be seen as 'in it for the money' which leads you to expect that someone else will negotiate for you; but no one negotiates on the part of the pastor, except the pastor. The problem being, as a new pastor you have little idea what you have signed up for or how it will impact your life and your family. No one prepares you for the fact that a pastor's life and his family's lives are fair game for discussion, for comment and for criticism. No one tells you that there are things that you should and shouldn't do—you largely work it out as you go along—and that in itself can be a painful journey.

What we have here in this excellent book is an attempt to rectify those issues. It is a helpful, often amusing, but sadly needed look at the pitfalls that many pastors face, with helpful thoughts about the paths through. This book should be read by those thinking of going into the ministry, by those beginning their ministry, and by any in leadership of churches seeking to appoint a minister. It will help to navigate through some thorny issues and in God's grace do it in a way that honours the Lord.

Simeon Woodcraft

(Simeon has been the pastor of New Milton Evangelical Free Church in Hampshire for the last seventeen years. He has also spent time training pastors in Uganda with *Equipping Pastors Worldwide*.)

8 The Pastorate

Contents

Commendations	**5**
Introduction	**11**
My background	13
My personality	19
The church	26
My ministry	30
1. First things first	**37**
Contract and stipend	37
Preaching	39
2. The important ones	**45**
My wife	45
The predecessor	47
Elders and deacons	54
The treasurer	61
Volunteers	65
3. Treading on eggshells	**68**
Music	68
Members' meetings	72
Charismatic issues	74
Women	76
Visiting missionaries	78
Sabbatical	81

Contents

4. So-called 'friendly fire' — **85**
   Conflict between members — 85
   Spitters and head shakers — 90
   Christmas trees — 92
   Criticism and false accusations — 95
   Words — 101

5. Battles within — **104**
   Temptation — 104
   Boredom — 107
   Anger and unforgiveness — 109
   A sense of humour — 112
   Alone but not lonely — 116
   When God seems to be absent — 119

6. What's the response? — **123**
   Church discipline — 123
   Numbers — 126
   When people leave — 130

7. Afterword — **134**

Introduction

I'm going to be writing about my own experiences in the pastorate, with all its ups and downs, although I'll be concentrating mainly on the downs. In one sense we can all cope with the good times and blessings that we receive. What tests us is when things go wrong, or when something happens that causes us anxiety and hurt. How do we respond to poison pen letters? To members who refuse to submit to our authority as pastor? To those who cry, 'Unless the pastor goes, I go'? To a group in the church (large or small) who are for ever criticising our preaching? To individuals who, for reasons best known to themselves, attempt to stir up the church against us? It is situations like the ones mentioned above that cause us to cry, 'Help, Lord, what do I do?' So I shall be focusing on the darker times that I assume most pastors experience at some time during their pastorates.

My purpose in doing so is not to discourage potential or serving pastors, but to offer a reality check. Even as a mature man entering the pastorate for the first time I had various ideals and ambitions about how I was going to turn the church around for good and to see it grow until we were bursting at the seams. I did tend to wear rose coloured glasses, thinking that I could succeed where others had failed.

In this work I want to offer some straightforward advice, born from my own experiences. I want to help those who might be struggling in the pastorate, and even thinking of quitting. I want to help those who are seriously thinking about becoming pastors and to get them to consider some of the pitfalls that might lie ahead. This may include those who have recently left Bible College and are looking for a church, or it may include someone who is more mature. It seems to me that more and more men are becoming pastors later in life after they have had many years of life experiences. There are many advantages to entering the pastorate at a later

Introduction

age, but it does not mean we will be guaranteed a trouble-free journey. Sometimes older men are more set in their ways and cannot adapt as easily as younger men.

Obviously everything I say is from my own perspective and it is not a 'must do for all'. I simply want to throw out a few ideas and lessons that I have learnt along the way. I am certainly not an 'expert', but I will endeavour to be completely open, frank and honest in what I say. In this I shall be like Oliver Cromwell, who demanded of the man who was going to paint his portrait that he wanted to be painted 'warts and all'; nothing must be left out. Inevitably you will not agree with everything I say or the conclusions I come to, and some of my thoughts may be controversial, but if it makes you think about possible solutions, then I have achieved my purpose.

I have omitted all personal names so as not to reveal an individual's identity; my purpose is not to offend anyone. But, other than that, all the details and events that I describe are one hundred percent accurate from my point of view. I relate them as they happened. My story is inevitably personal and the advice I pass on is both practical and spiritual. The pastorate is a practical profession, as well as a spiritual calling, with all sorts of practical decisions and arrangements that have to be made.

One of my motivations in writing has been to remind my readers that the pastorate is not an easy position to fill. I smiled when I read this description of a pastor's life:

'The pastor teaches, though he must gather his own classes. He heals, though without medicines or a knife. He is sometimes a lawyer, often a social worker, something of an editor, a bit of a philosopher and entertainer. He is a salesman, an administrator, a decorative piece at public functions and he is supposed to be a scholar. He visits the sick, marries those in love, buries the dead, labours to console the grieving and to admonish those who sin. He tries to remain sweet when accused of not doing his duty. He plans programmes, appoints committees (when he can get them) and spends considerable time in keeping people out of each other's hair. In between times he prepares sermons and preaches them on Sundays to those who don't happen to have any other engagements. Then on Monday, as he is recovering from the previous day's exertions, he smiles pleasantly at some jovial chap who roars out, "It's all right for some who only work one day a week!"'

Well, I think that just about says it all!

My background

Perhaps the best way to start is to give a little personal background. Before entering the pastorate I was in education for twenty-five years, thirteen of which was as a teaching head of a primary school. It was a job I loved and couldn't wait to restart after the long school holidays. I did some lay preaching 'on the side', but I was never particularly bothered about how much I preached, although I read a lot about preaching and preachers, and even spent many years researching in great detail several of the more well-known preachers. I also read a great deal about the pastorate, but had no interest or desire to become a pastor, in spite of several people encouraging me to consider such a calling.

After I had been teaching for about twenty years, for some unknown reason I started to receive more opportunities to preach. These were unsolicited and I felt that I should accept them as part of my service to God. After a while I found that I wanted more of these opportunities to come along and prayed accordingly. One of the churches I went to on a regular basis was the church I would eventually pastor. They had been given my name by someone who had heard me preach. As this church was in the middle of an interregnum I was invited there quite often, sometimes for about six or seven weeks in a row, morning and evening. They obviously liked my ministry because quite early on they asked if I was looking for a position in a church, to which I said, 'No thank you.'

My view had always been that the last thing I wanted to do was to become a pastor, telling my friends that the reason for this decision was

Introduction

because I did not want a nervous breakdown! This was said partly 'tongue in cheek', but partly from what I had seen and heard. I knew too many pastors who had had serious problems with their health and mental state owing to the stresses and strains of the pastorate. And that was not for me. Besides, I was happy in my job and earning a decent salary, so why would I want to change all that for what I thought was a life of hardship, pain and sacrifice? Sorry if that doesn't sound very spiritual! I suppose I was stuck in my comfort zone.

What I didn't know at the time was that the more I preached at this church the more the congregation wanted me as their pastor, and some, in various church meetings, became quite forthright in their support of me. Unbeknown to me at the time, some were even praying over that verse in Proverbs 21:1: 'The king's heart is in the hand of the Lord; he directs it like a watercourse wherever he pleases.' They were asking God to change my heart and move it towards becoming their pastor. I don't think I would have been too pleased if I'd known what they were up to!

After I had preached there about fifty times or more as a supply preacher I started to feel unsettled at school. There was nothing in particular that was happening, certainly nothing out of the ordinary, but I started to think seriously to myself, 'Well, I've been teaching for some twenty-five years; is this what I want to do for the rest of my working life?' For some reason that seemed an awfully long time. 'Was it time for a change?' I asked myself. I started to wrestle with the idea of pursuing a different direction in my life, which turned into a kind of 'mid-life crisis', although I had always thought that was something that only women experienced! Subsequently I have spoken to quite a few men who have gone through something similar.

I began to think incessantly about a new challenge. What would it be like? How would I cope stepping out of the rather comfortable life I had built for myself? I thought about the pastorate and serving God in the church, and it didn't seem quite so horrendous. Actually, if I'm totally honest, I began to warm to the idea, which worried me enormously because of my long-standing negative attitude to such a position. Enthusiastic would be too strong a word at this stage, but that was the direction in which I was heading.

At the same time I started to suffer from insomnia. Since attending boarding school from the age of ten I have always been rather anxious about getting to sleep, but I had up to that point never suffered from insomnia. Again there was no particular reason for this, but it was devastating. I remember one occasion, after trying to get to sleep for four or five hours sitting on the end of the bed, banging it hard with my fist in utter frustration, with my wife looking on in a sympathetic but somewhat helpless manner. I just could not sleep until about six in the morning, and then I got up at seven and went off to run a school and teach lively ten and eleven-year-olds on just one hour's sleep. I distinctly remember in the morning, in my zombie state, as I stepped into the kitchen, envying my two cats who were curled up fast asleep. 'Oh, if only I were a cat,' I'd sigh! For the first time in my teaching career I found it difficult to control the children. The doctor gave me some sleeping tablets, which helped a little.

Looking back I can now see that the Lord was 'stirring up my rather comfortable nest'. I had always thought I would be teaching until retirement age and it had all become a little too easy for me. Over the years I had met all the challenges of modern teaching and had coped with the stresses and strains of a headship. Working life had become too straightforward and familiar for me. Little did I know at that time, but a new challenge was on the horizon and maybe the prayer of the congregation over Proverbs 21:1 was being answered.

In this unsettled state I went to talk with two pastors, one retired, the other a local pastor whose church was about three miles from where I lived. I wanted to know what they thought of the possibility of my becoming a pastor. We chatted. They went away and listened to some of my sermons and were favourable in their response that the pastorate was something they thought I should explore. I asked one of the men to be my mentor and we met on a weekly basis to talk about the pastorate.

Introduction

After a while I went to the main deacon at the church where I had been preaching a great deal to say that I was thinking about the pastorate, and were they still interested? Well, the deacon almost took it as though I had already signed the contract! I suddenly felt fearful that I was being pushed into something that I didn't really want to do. Help! How do I get out of this one? Suddenly the words from *Laurel and Hardy* came into my mind: 'This is another nice mess you've got me into!'

I had some serious thinking and praying to do. What did God want me to do? How could I discover his will? Somewhat confused, I laid it all before my Saviour. I can't say I ever got a flash of light to point me in the right direction, or even a specific word from the Bible, but slowly I was coming round to the 'terrifying' idea of becoming a pastor. I even felt quite enthusiastic about the prospect, which surprised me.

As I was not one hundred percent sure about my future I put a proposal to the church via one of their deacons. I would happily take on all the responsibilities of the pastorate for ten months. After that time, if I or the church felt that it was not working out, then either side could say 'no thanks' and walk away without any further ado. Maybe I was secretly hoping that this would be unacceptable to the church and therefore they would say no and I would have no decision to make. I would return to teaching as if nothing had happened.

Unfortunately they were delighted with the proposal and began to draw up a ten month contract. I say 'unfortunately' with a bit of a cheeky grin as by this time I was growing more positive about this new role. I was still fearful, but God had changed my heart enough for me to 'give it a go'. Rather than saying 'no way' to the pastorate, I was thinking, 'Maybe I could do this. In fact, I *want* to do this!' Again this does not sound very spiritual, and it's certainly not what is written in the books about becoming a pastor. I expect someone like Richard Baxter, the author of *The Reformed Pastor*, would be turning in his grave; but all I can do is tell the truth and let the reader judge it in the way he or she sees fit.

The role of my wife at this uncertain time was also significant. At first she tended to laugh off any talk about the pastorate, knowing my previous feelings towards it. Whenever we discussed the matter, she would only mention the negative aspects of such a life and do all she could to dissuade me from even thinking about such a possibility. She certainly could not imagine herself as a pastor's wife. This went on for quite a while; then suddenly, almost overnight, her opinion altered and she started to encourage me along that path. Such a change not only shocked me, but panicked me. 'Is this another sign that God wants me to become a pastor?' I wondered. 'Was I being pushed into a corner? Is it now too late to stick to teaching?'

In the middle of all these 'wonderings about my future' a very interesting event took place. My deputy had worked with me at the same school for about twenty years. She was a lovely Christian lady and we had an excellent working relationship. She had never mentioned any desire to be the head of the school and I had not mentioned anything to her about the decisions I had been battling with over the pastorate.

One day out of the blue she came to me and said, 'Do you know what happened to me on Sunday morning as I was listening to the sermon?' Of course I had no idea. 'I suddenly felt God say to me in no uncertain terms that I could run the school. That I could become the head teacher.' I dread to think of the way I looked at her, but it was almost as if she had known all along what had been going on in my own mind and life, which of course was impossible. Later she confirmed that she had no idea what I had been up to or praying about.

In many ways that dealt with some of the big questions I had in my own mind: Who would take over from me as head if I left? How much notice would the school require? How long would it take to go through the whole process of finding a new leader? And now the Lord had just handed to me my replacement on a plate. I must admit it was a bit scary, but it was exciting at the same time. Does this really mean God wants me to be a pastor? Will I have a nervous breakdown? Why does God want me

Introduction

to do something I have always dreaded? For me, my deputy's 'revelation' was the final nail in the coffin of all my arguments about escaping the pastorate. It was soon afterwards that I made my ten-month proposal to the church.

Lessons

What are some of the lessons that I learned from all my 'to-ing and fro-ing'?

- The first one must be that God's word is true. Proverbs 16:1 says: 'To man belong the plans of the heart, but from the Lord comes the reply of the tongue.' Or a few verses on it says: 'In his heart a man plans his course, but the Lord determines his steps' (Proverbs 16:9). I had planned my course of staying in teaching until my retirement, but it was the Lord who showed me the way to go.

- God is sovereign and will have his way in our lives. Sometimes we fight and try to go our own way, but the Lord's purpose will prevail. 'Many are the plans in a man's heart, but it is the Lord's purpose that prevails' (Proverbs 19:21). He is in control. He will direct our paths. As Spurgeon said, 'If God lights the candle, none can blow it out.' Therefore we need not fear.

- God uses other people to accomplish his purposes for us. He used my deputy to push me down the road he wanted me to travel. He used my wife to encourage me towards the pastorate, in spite of her initial reservations. He used two pastors to counsel and advise me in the right direction. He used the enthusiasm and prayers of the church to change my mind.

- God will sometimes stir up our nests if they become too comfortable. I'm not saying he will always do such a thing, but he will sometimes.

He will use hardships to speak to us. He used my insomnia to grab my attention and to speak to me and to close the door on teaching. As my favourite Puritan writer Thomas Watson says, 'When God lays men upon their backs, then they look up to heaven.'

- Martin Luther said that adversity was the best book in his library. It is said that the greater the weight that is laid upon a palm tree, or hung to its branches, the more it grows and flourishes. So although difficulties and suffering are never pleasant, they can produce an abundance of fruit. The Psalms were born from David's pain. 'There is a pain that is productive of life itself' (Eric Alexander).

- If we are honestly wanting God's will, we do not have to be afraid that we might miss it. God will not send us down a wrong road. He will guide us down paths of righteousness for his name's sake. The Lord will get us to our destination even if our sinful natures are kicking and screaming; even if our minds are confused about which way to turn; even if the advice we receive is contrary to God's plan.

- The Lord answers prayer. Although I was not the one praying over Proverbs 21:1, members of the church were and God heard and answered their prayer for me. This gives us great encouragement to continue praying for others. Perhaps the words of Samuel Rutherford are applicable here: 'I seldom made an errand to God for another but I got something for myself.'

My personality

The next subject we must talk about is my personality. Was I suited to the pastorate? If I'm brutally honest, I don't think my personality and temperament were ideally suited to such a role. But there again, how would we describe the perfect pastoral temperament? We're told that a pastor needs a skin like a rhinoceros on the one hand and great sensitivity

Introduction

on the other: the rhinoceros skin because of all the 'comments' that are made to and about him, and the sensitivity because of the empathy and understanding he has to show to those who are hurting.

The rhinoceros skin is something I don't have. I'm sensitive, perhaps too sensitive about little things such as someone's body language or tone of voice or facial expression. I had a verse pinned to the wall in my study which read in the AV: 'Be not afraid of their faces, for I am with thee to deliver thee, saith the Lord' (Jeremiah 1:8). I found that when I was preaching an angry look or a scowl or frown from someone in the congregation could be disconcerting. The first time I went to preach at a hospital for the mentally ill, there was someone in the small congregation who kept shaking his head at everything I said, which I found quite off-putting. I thought to myself, 'What am I saying that he doesn't like?' After the meeting I discovered that this man was actually one of the Christian team that went into the hospital every month. He had something wrong with his neck, so to show his appreciation he had to shake his head rather than nod. So all the time I was speaking he was agreeing with me! I must admit I felt a bit of an idiot for being so sensitive, but it's hard to change one's nature.

Another illustration might help at this point to show that we cannot tell from people's faces how they are feeling or what they are thinking. It concerns an American missionary to India by the name of David Grant. He was a man bursting with so much energy, especially when he preached, that he literally could not contain it. He once told me that he went to preach at a Dutch Reformed Church of the old school. The members were extremely strict, never displayed any emotion in church and seemed to be 'as hard as nails' as they listened to him. As he was preaching he became so excited that he actually ran round the church three times during his sermon, shouting. Apparently not a single person in the congregation moved a muscle during this exhibition of enthusiasm! Their stony faces remained stony. At the close of the service he thought he was in for real trouble and prepared himself for a verbal lashing. To his surprise when the offering was taken for his work in India it was the largest he had ever received from a church of that size. One elderly lady came up to him at the end and said, 'Well, I didn't understand much of what you said, but I loved watching you worship God!' You see, we cannot tell what people are thinking from the expressions on their faces.

Having said all that, sensitivity is vital for a pastor—sensitivity towards people's feelings, opinions, the trials they are facing and so on. It is better to be sensitive than hard and seemingly uncaring. There are many times when we have to hurt with those who are hurting and weep with those who weep. Soon after I started at the church a middle-aged couple went on holiday to the north of Wales. Tragically, while there, the husband died suddenly. My wife and I rushed to that part of the country and were able to stand alongside her in the midst of her grief and to help her with many of the practical difficulties. The love and care we showed her in this time of need was never forgotten by her and she always held us in the highest regard.

I dislike confrontation, but at times in the pastorate you have to stand up for what you believe. You have to argue, sometimes vigorously, against a view or doctrine that you regard as unbiblical or at least unhelpful to the progress of the church. You may have to rebuke an individual for their behaviour or resist a group who don't approve of how you are leading the services. 'The fear of man is a snare', and one has to be ready to confront where necessary. This is something that doesn't come naturally, although there were several occasions when I did 'take on' someone who I felt was acting inappropriately and needed a good talking to about their behaviour. But it was not something I relished.

I am not in the mould of John Knox or Charles Spurgeon. Spurgeon once said, 'I have hardly ever known what the fear of man means.' That's not me. Most pastors get criticised, sometimes mercilessly, and even have enemies within the church. I spoke to one pastor after he had resigned his position and he told me that because of various things that had happened in his church some twenty-five members out of a congregation of about 110 completely blanked him. They refused to look at him or speak to

Introduction

him. They behaved as if he did not exist. Rather than confronting such behaviour, he left and took up lorry driving (literally). Thankfully nothing quite so extreme or disgraceful happened to me, but anything like that, if I'm not careful, sends me into my shell and I just want it to 'go away'.

I mentioned above that 'most pastors get criticised'—the key word being 'most'. I have a friend who remained in the pastorate just four years. The reason he left was not because of criticism, because nobody criticised him. In fact, nobody said anything to him good or bad. No one thanked him, or challenged him or commented on his sermons or gave an opinion on anything he ever did. His congregation were entirely passive about everything he did or wanted to do. From his first day to his last he never knew if people appreciated his ministry or hated it! Such silence and indifference drove him out of the pastorate.

Although outwardly I give the impression of being a confident person, inwardly I'm rather reserved. That's why I don't find it easy to stand up in front of people to preach. That might sound a bit strange for a teacher and a preacher, but even George Whitefield found it difficult. I would prefer to sit in the background rather than have everyone's eyes on me. I can be a little insecure and sometimes need reassurance that what I am doing is right and in the best interest of everyone concerned. In the pastorate, as in most other positions of responsibility, criticism seems to come more easily than commendation. It seems people will write a letter to show how much they disagree with what you are doing, but will not pick up a pen when they appreciate your work. Can I just say at this point that I received more criticism in the first three months of the pastorate than I ever did in twenty-five years as a teacher. Now that's a sad picture of the attitude of some church members. Like most pastors, I work best when I feel loved and appreciated, when I know the congregation is rooting for me, praying for me, supporting me, rather than criticising me or opposing me.

I am quite a private person, and so having to 'tell all' to the congregation—all about your children, where you are going on holiday, what you did on your day off, what time you get up and go to bed and so on—felt a bit like an unwanted intrusion and an invasion of privacy. I would perhaps go so far as to say that I'm not really a people person. I like people, and I enjoy talking about a serious subject and having a good laugh, but I'm not particularly gifted at 'small talk'. I remember a well-known preacher saying to me that pastors need to be skilled at 'small talk' to make people feel at ease and because it can lead to 'big talk' about important subjects. That's not one of my gifts. I find 'small talk' difficult. I'm not naturally chatty. I don't have the gift of the gab. I would almost describe myself as shy, although I can put on a show of sociability and 'talk a good talk' when necessary.

Nor would I put empathy at the top of my personality traits, although I am a caring person. Now that might sound like a contradiction! What I am trying to say is that I do care, but I tend to be too impatient, especially if in my opinion someone is making a 'fuss about nothing'. I try to understand and to show sympathy, but it does not always come easily. I find it more natural to advise and instruct.

Perhaps at this stage it would only be fair to myself to mention some positive characteristics of my personality. Even the weakest personality has strengths. I will do this briefly as the whole premise of my book is to dwell on the negative.

I'm an organised, self-disciplined and hardworking person. I always have been since I've been a Christian. I'm efficient. I hate leaving anything undone or unanswered on my desk. I can't stand having work 'hanging over me'. Any problem that arises I try to sort out immediately, dealing with each point as fully and conscientiously as I can, leaving nothing out. Sometimes I feel a bit like a friend of mine. Whenever he is given a plate of food, say chicken, chips, peas and carrots, he first of all eats the peas, then the carrots, then the chips before he eats the meat. That's what I do with my work. I take each bit and deal with it before I move on. I am systematic.

I'm a good listener. In fact, I think I prefer listening to talking (now that's rare!). I fully concentrate on what someone is saying without

Introduction

getting distracted, unlike those annoying people who look around the room when you're sharing a problem with them, giving the impression they are not really interested. I then make what I have heard a matter of sincere prayer.

I have a devotional frame of mind and usually have lengthy times of prayer. It is extremely unusual for me to miss out on a daily devotional time. For me prayer is a top priority. It's a lifeline to my Saviour. This in turn keeps my conscience tender and has led to a desire to serve the Lord in whatever capacity he sees fit. If he opens a door, I'll do my utmost to walk through it.

I'm quite good at finding practical solutions to problems. Any counsel I give is usually 'sound' and appreciated. I can fairly easily see behind a façade and discover what the 'real' problem is and what to do about it. From all my reading and study I have a wealth of knowledge to draw on and years of practical experience from my headship. Speaking of problems reminds me of what Albert Einstein said, 'A clever person solves a problem. A wise person avoids it.'

You might ask, 'Well, what is the *principal* gift you have that is suitable to the pastorate?' I have the ability to teach. I can teach clearly and succinctly. That's my strength. I can take some complicated doctrine or theological issue and break it down to bite-size pieces so even the most unlettered can understand. I did that kind of thing for twenty-five years with children. And I can do the same with adults. I can make myself easily understood. There is little ambiguity or confusion in what I say. When I preach, people know exactly what I am saying. And they seemed to appreciate that.

I can at times be extremely bold when preaching, and the fear of man just disappears. Occasionally, when under the anointing of God's Spirit and with a divine authority, I have even surprised myself at some of the things I have uttered. I have been like an Old Testament prophet! This holy boldness inevitably causes a reaction, sometimes positive, sometimes negative. I was once preaching on Zephaniah 1:14–18 and emphasising with force the day of God's wrath before a congregation of many hundreds. One member of that congregation was obviously gripped by what I said and came to the church office the following day, crying out in panic, 'That sermon, that sermon! I can't escape from it! I've got to get right with the Lord.' There and then the staff member led him to Christ.

I think logically. The points of my sermons are digestible. You can take them home with you. I saw one member of my old church over two years after I had resigned and she told me that when she could not make it to church the other week she listened to one of my old sermons. Her comment to me was, 'Why did we ever let you leave?' So teaching is my principal gift.

Lessons

- You don't have to be a perfect individual to enter the pastorate. You don't have to possess all the gifts you think are necessary for such a position. Of course our congregations would like that, even expect it, but we can't all be a Charles Spurgeon, George Whitefield and Martyn Lloyd-Jones rolled into one. God uses cracked vessels. Can you think of a pastor who is massively gifted in every area? Probably not. Your present pastor is almost certainly more gifted in some areas and less so in others. That's just how it is. None of us is perfect and we should not beat ourselves up because we fall short in some areas.

- God can still use you even if you are imperfect. He uses weak people, unlikely people, people who can't tick all the boxes and present a long list of wonderful qualifications, whose personality CV is not full of confidence, strong leadership qualities and the ability to comfort all who mourn. In spite of all my weaknesses God still used me, as we shall see as this book unfolds. Remember that Paul said 'I will boast all the more gladly about my weaknesses, so that Christ's power may rest on me … for when I am weak, then I am strong.' God's power is made perfect in weakness (2 Corinthians 12:8–10).

Introduction

- Work hard on your weaknesses so they become stronger. Don't just throw in the towel and say, 'This is how I am and I cannot change.' God is able to help, to strengthen. If your preaching is your weak point, study hard to improve it. Ask God to anoint you with his Spirit. Cry out to him to make it more effective. If like me you are not very sympathetic, plead with God to soften your heart and to give you more understanding and grace. Be like the top footballers who work hard to improve their weaker foot.

- Try to encourage others who are struggling because they think everything they do is sub-standard. I remember going to a pastors' conference and while in the toilet (can you believe it) getting into a serious conversation with another pastor. He started to unburden his heart to me. I didn't dare suggest a change of location in case it broke the thread of what he was saying. So we stayed in the toilet for a good thirty to forty minutes chatting. Amazingly no one else came in during that time, so we had some privacy! But he seemed depressed and ready to give up because things were not going well in his church. I encouraged him to focus on Christ and what he can do rather than on his own weaknesses and failings. I'm not sure if I helped him much, but I tried.

- If God has called you to the pastorate, do your best. Give yourself fully to your calling, with all your weaknesses, and leave room for God to do his work. Remember, without Jesus we can do nothing (John 15:5). And remember your work in the Lord is never in vain (1 Corinthians 15:58).

The church

The church I went to was a traditional reformed independent church, which was affiliated to the FIEC (Fellowship of Independent Evangelical Churches). It had two services on a Sunday and a mid-week Bible study and prayer meeting. The organ was played most Sunday mornings and the piano in the evenings. The main hymn book was the old *Christian Hymns* with a copy of the *Mission Praise* hymnbook for a backup. The previous minister had been there for nearly thirty years. He had been ill for the last year of his pastorate after which the church had had a two-year interregnum. The Sunday morning congregation numbered about twenty members, all but three of whom were beyond the age of retirement. (Interestingly, the younger members had the attitude and outlook of the over 80s!) There were few visitors on a Sunday and probably three or four regular non-members. The numbers on Sunday evening were slightly lower. The Sunday school consisted of three children, all of whom were brought by their grandparents, and there were no young families in the church.

The church had the reputation of being old-fashioned. Some would say, rather unkindly, that it was 'stuck in the eighteenth century'. The format of the services was the hymn/sandwich type with little variation. When I arrived the general atmosphere was a bit 'down in the dumps' and the congregation was rudderless and discouraged. In other words, it was typical of a church that had been effectively without a pastor for three years. Those who had not left were the faithful ones who were prepared to stick with the church come what may. They were wanting a man to revive their fortunes and to bring new life to a dying cause.

There were five deacons and no elder. There was no website, no church policies and, as far as I can remember, no one had had a DBS check (the old CRB checks). The church building was about twenty-five years old, so it was fairly modern with a good-sized hall at the back. The eighty individual seats were comfortable and could be moved. There was no office at the church although there was the possibility of changing one of the store rooms into an office. There was parking for about seven cars.

The congregation could easily be split in two. The congenial part (about seventy percent of the membership) was made up mainly but not entirely of elderly ladies, who were gracious and sweet and who would go along with about ninety percent of anything that happened without question or

Introduction

complaint. They did not resist any change and were supportive throughout my time at the church. Within this group were those who wanted the church to become more modern and suitable for the twenty-first century in the hope that a younger congregation could be attracted to attend. At times they would push gently for various modernisations, always in a godly and inoffensive manner.

The remaining thirty percent, while being committed Christians with a desire to be holy, were more vocal and opinionated. They were happy with how the church functioned and had imbibed the theology and methods of the previous pastor. They had strong views as to how a church should operate, were resistant of any change, clung rigidly to *Christian Hymns* and the organ, and hated anything that in their view had the slightest whiff of the Charismatic church. At times some were aggressive, awkward and unwilling to submit to any suggested change made by their new pastor.

They reminded me of the story John Benton tells in his excellent book *The big picture for small churches*: 'I can vividly remember being confronted by an older lady soon after I arrived in the ministry. One Sunday she came into the vestry, with her walking stick held tightly in her hand, and closed the door behind her. She had got me alone. She looked at me with steely eyes and said, "You won't change anything, will you?" When I was unable to give her that assurance I was rather worried what she might do with the walking stick!' (p. 28). Well, John survived, but it will give you a flavour of some of the members in my new church.

What I did not know when I arrived was that the tension between these two groups had manifested itself at various times in the past and there had been periods of serious conflict. It seems as though the previous minister had tried to steer a middle course, although he leaned towards favouring the second group in order to avoid unnecessary trouble. The bottom line in all this was that, as far as I could tell, nothing much had really changed in the last thirty years because the second group were more forthright in putting forward their views.

Lessons

- Learn as much about the church as possible *before* you become the pastor. Ask yourself if it is the kind of church that will fit in with your views and vice versa. Try to understand the congregation and whether it will be possible to lead them in the direction you want them to go. If you have a question and answer session before your appointment, use it to ask as many questions as you answer. There is no point going to a church that is theologically different from your own standpoint or one that has a completely different methodology.

- Speak frankly with the leadership team and if possible with the outgoing pastor. They may not want to hang out all the dirty washing, but try to understand the history of the church and the problems that have occurred in the past. One of my deacons spoke to me openly about the difficulties and was a fount of information. Unfortunately he did not tell me about 'all the warts' until after my appointment.

- Of course no church is perfect, just like no pastor is perfect, but is there hope that your ideas and the direction you want to lead the church (your vision), if handled wisely, will be embraced? Will change be possible or impossible? How much pain will it cause?

- If you want to make sudden and rather drastic changes, be ready for a battle. Remember that some older people live in the past and find change genuinely difficult. Be sympathetic towards their views but don't let them prevent you from doing what is best for the church.

- In my experience it is extremely difficult to change a church if a large proportion of the congregation will not allow it. You can use all your charm and persuasive powers but to no avail. Either the pastor ends up

Introduction

leaving or a significant percentage of the congregation leaves, which can be 'life-threatening' to a small church.

- I like what Vance Havner says, which should be the bedrock of your ministry: 'The church has no greater need today than to fall in love with Jesus all over again.'

My ministry

It's probably best to say that my ministry can be divided into three periods. The first period was what is often referred to as the 'honeymoon'. Mine was perhaps longer than some, for it lasted over two years. During that time the congregation were supportive. I was happy and fulfilled in the ministry and the Lord's blessing was on the church. During those two years we had 26 new members, which more than doubled the membership. For a small church that was remarkable. About 70 attended in the morning and 40 in the evening. The prayer meeting was a real encouragement, with some 35 to 40 members praying and with no long gaps between the prayers. A missionary couple who spoke at the church on an annual basis said they had not experienced such a lively prayer meeting in any other church they had visited. We also enjoyed regular weeks of prayer, which were well attended and well received.

During those years I felt assured of God's call on my life and was really enjoying my new role. I even wrote to the deacons and said that I thought the Lord had been preparing me all my life for this opportunity and was quite ready to stay until retirement. When an FIEC representative came to the church I told him how much I was enjoying being a pastor (I learned later that this representative had himself left the pastorate because 'it had nearly killed him'). I honestly could not see anything disturbing this 'heavenly experience'.

My walk with the Lord was intimate and fulfilling. I usually spent up to two hours in prayer each day and read quite a few chapters of the Bible. On Saturday evenings I had an additional time with the Lord to prepare for Sundays. I started about 5 pm and finished about 7 pm, but this was later extended to 11 pm with an hour in between for my evening meal. My time included an hour prayer walk, reading a couple of sermons (usually Martyn Lloyd-Jones), Bible reading and other spiritually beneficial exercises. I know not everyone can spend this length of time in devotions, so I don't want to turn this into a legalistic exercise or a guilt trip. Even my mentor told me not to 'overdo it or be too spiritual!' But for me it was something I enjoyed and looked forward to each week. When times became more difficult, I found I was praying for even longer, pouring out my troubles to the Lord.

If I was to criticise myself in this area, I would say that self-effort rather than relying on the Lord was often my motivation. Maybe I tried too hard, which had a detrimental effect on me when things started to go wrong. I have always found the distinction between faith and works difficult. We of course need to work hard, but we need to fully trust the Lord in every area and rely on his power to accomplish his purposes.

An illustration may help. A Christian man used to row people across a river in Scotland. That was his job. On one oar he carved the word 'works' and on the other oar he carved the word 'faith'. One day a passenger asked him about the two words. Before saying anything he pulled in the 'works' oar and rowed only with the 'faith' oar. The boat just went round in circles and made no progress. He then pulled in the 'faith' oar and rowed only with the 'works' oar. The same thing happened, except he was going round in circles in the opposite direction. He then rowed with both oars and got his passenger safely to the other side. As his passenger departed he said to him, 'In order to get safely to heaven's shore, we need both faith and works.' Keeping these two in harmony and correctly balanced in the Christian life needs both skill and wisdom.

Now I have carefully looked back and analysed what changed over the coming years. Why did I go from pure enjoyment to struggling in a relatively short time, in a matter of about six months? I have thought and thought about this, but cannot put my finger on any one event or situation.

Introduction

It would be much easier for me to understand if I could. But I can't. Of course, we must never forget the spiritual battle we are in and our terrible adversary. Undoubtedly he had a part to play. But sometimes he is hard to recognise and resist. What I do know for sure comes from a letter I wrote to a retired pastor whose advice I was seeking. In this letter I mentioned several issues with which I was struggling. This is how I opened my letter: 'When I analyse the problems, I see three things working together—my own temperament, which tends to aggravate the difficulties (I am too intense about things and tend to drive myself unnecessarily, feeling guilty if I'm not working incessantly for the church); the discipline of the Lord, who is painfully shaping me into his image; and the attacks of the devil.'

I go on to mention incessant sermon preparation. It was at this stage in my pastorate that I started to struggle with such questions as: 'What is the point of preaching three times a week to the same congregation? Do the members need so many sermons? Are they doing them any good? Are they growing spiritually and becoming more Christ-like as a result? Is the only benefit to keep them on the straight and narrow until they reach heaven?' I think these questions that I found hard to answer had a debilitating effect on me psychologically.

In the letter I mentioned a lack of fellowship and depression as further reasons why I felt like 'throwing in the towel'. I also said that 'I have no complaints about the church itself or about the people in it, who are very appreciative and caring. The leaders are supportive and we have a good relationship.' So in a relatively short time things went downhill. It is actually quite scary to think how quickly this all happened and without a specific reason why.

So what do you do in a situation like that? The retired pastor, while being sympathetic, had no easy solution. All I can remember him saying is that perhaps I should get some help, an assistant to work alongside me, for company, encouragement and a sharing of the workload. Easier said than done. It certainly would not be an instant fix. When I mentioned an assistant to the leadership they were broadly supportive, but a group within the congregation could not understand why I needed help. Their attitude tended to be: 'You are getting paid to do a job. Get on with it. We cannot afford to pay anyone else' (which was not actually true as the church had plenty of money).

Let me say in passing that what I have just described is a common scenario, particularly for pastors of smaller churches where they have no other member who is employed by the church. Such a situation tends to lead to a sort of spiritual isolation, where molehills can become mountains because there is no one else with whom to discuss all the situations that arise on a daily basis. Many of these issues will be discussed in later chapters. So I sum up this second period by saying I was battling against myself.

The third period of my ministry can be summarised under the heading: 'When things started to go wrong in the church,' or, 'When I was battling against others'—things such as opposition to my ministry from a minority; people leaving; my only elder siding with a member of the congregation against me; conflict between members; false accusations; open criticism; and so on. Instead of trying to understand the problems I was facing and giving me a helping hand, a few of the members blamed me personally. Looking back, some of the congregation could be described as 'fair weather friends'.

Now I am not saying in all this that I was the perfect pastor. Far from it! But I honestly did try to do what was right in God's sight, to be gracious in my responses and not to over-react. The more problems occurred, the more I prayed. I tended to withdraw from people and did my utmost to avoid conflict. But the more I did that, the worse things became. I suppose by this stage I did not have all the necessary energy to fight my corner. If I did step over the mark and react in an ungracious manner—and at times I did in the way I handled people—I castigated myself ruthlessly.

The final straw that broke the camel's back was when a mature couple I had recently married came to me on a Saturday night (as I was preparing for Sunday) and told me they were out of fellowship with me. I asked them

Introduction

why that was and what I had done as I was ready to apologise, but they said I hadn't done anything wrong. I was a bit lost for words. Further questioning just confirmed that I had not done anything to upset them yet they were 'out of fellowship' with me. I was confused. I could hardly believe what I was hearing or not hearing. We prayed together and they left. The following Tuesday I resigned.

You might think that was all rather trivial, and taken in isolation I agree with you. But it was the final straw. If you keep adding straws, eventually even the strongest back will break. By that stage I had lost all hope and was a broken man. And that was the end of my ministry at that church.

Now you might be tempted to conclude that I probably brought a lot of the troubles on myself. I would certainly agree that I didn't always handle situations and people wisely. Maybe I would have approached some things differently with hindsight or more maturity and grace. But it is true to say that many of the problems were already in the church when I first arrived but were kept hidden for quite a while. One of my members, who had been in the church during the difficult times, and as a full time Christian worker had experienced all sorts of churches, said to me several years after I had left, in reference to the difficulties: 'Not all churches are like your church. I've never experienced before what I experienced in your church.'

Before I left some in the church realised they had not treated me as they should have done, and one member of the newly formed search committee for the new pastor said to me in one meeting, 'I think we owe you an apology.' This was in response to a booklet that the search committee had received from the FIEC about how to treat your pastor. I think they realised that many of its recommendations had not been implemented as far as I was concerned. Another former member came back to the church one Sunday specifically to apologise to me (in fact he came back twice!) because he knew it was wrong to oppose an elder as he had done without good reason.

Lessons

- Rejoice in the good times. Make the most of them. Thank God for them, because harder times might be just around the corner.

- Never underestimate the role of Satan in attacking pastors, especially when your ministry is being blessed. Our enemy will not sit around and idly watch God at work. Be ever vigilant. Ask God to give you the spirit of discernment that you might be able to spot the schemes of the devil. Be alert and self-controlled (1 Peter 5:8). Remember 'our struggle is not against flesh and blood, but against the rulers, against the authorities, against the powers of this dark world and against the spiritual forces of evil in the heavenly realms' (Ephesians 6:12). It was only after I had left the church that I saw more clearly what the devil had been up to during my pastorate and how he had used different people in different ways.

- A saying of George Swinnock's is meaningful to me when I consider my isolation in the pastorate and the possibilities that open up to the devil: 'Satan watches for those vessels that sail without a convoy.'

- Do not be surprised if white becomes black very quickly. One day the sun might be shining, the next day the storm arrives. There might be no logical reason for the change, but the change comes nevertheless. Joseph in the Old Testament was one day the pride and joy of his father, the next he was thrown into a cistern and sold into slavery. Jesus was hailed by the crowd on Palm Sunday and crucified a few days later. Try to prepare yourself for anything, but without worrying about the future.

- If, like me, you ever wonder what is the point of preaching so many times, then this story might help. When a local preacher died, his relatives found that all his old sermons had been tied together, with a note left on the top which read, 'Where has the influence gone of all

Introduction

these sermons that I preached?' Underneath he had scribbled the word 'over'. On the other side was this answer. 'Where are last year's sun rays? They have gone into fruits and grain and vegetables to feed mankind. Where are last year's raindrops? Forgotten by most, of course, but they accomplished their refreshing work, and their influence still abides.' The Lord is able to fulfil his purposes even through our sermons.

- An anonymous saying goes: 'God sometimes blesses a poor exegesis of a bad translation of a doubtful rendering of an obscure verse of a minor prophet!' If you haven't already, read the conversion story of Charles Spurgeon—not exactly the greatest preacher and the greatest sermon, yet Spurgeon was converted!

- The Lord will never disappoint us. Others might, but our Saviour is always trustworthy. Stand by him. Look to him. Depend on him. Follow the example of Jesus and never fully commit yourself into the hands of men. Rather, throw yourself on Christ. He alone is our hope, our salvation.

- Pray without ceasing. Whatever happens, keep close to the Lord in prayer. Don't let anyone or anything cut off your source of life and hope. When the going gets tough, run to your shepherd. When in trouble, pray. If isolated, pray. When confused, pray. When criticised, pray.

1. First things first

In everything mentioned below, I relate my own personal experience first and then offer a few practical points at the end of each section, some of which can be put down to the wisdom of hindsight. Let's begin with two of the most important areas of church life: the contract and preaching.

The contract and stipend

The contract is something you must try to get right before you sign it, because it is notoriously difficult to change once agreed. It is also a legal document which members of the church may get to read and therefore comment on, as I discovered. Don't feel ashamed or embarrassed or think it is unspiritual to negotiate a better 'deal' for yourself. You are the one who will have to live with it for many years. On the whole, I was happy with my contract, although I should not have settled for such a low stipend. I was paid considerably less than what was recommended by the FIEC and it was afterwards impossible to get a yearly increase much above the rate of inflation. This meant my stipend was consistently below other similar pastors in my area. I lived in my own house, which I used as my office, but did not receive any allowance for electricity, gas, etc., and I had no pension from the church. In hindsight my stipend was something I should have negotiated more keenly, especially as the church had plenty of money. However, the book allowance was generous, I was allowed six weeks' holiday a year (I was used to 17 weeks' holiday as a teacher!) and encouraged to attend two conferences of my choice. Two weeks for study leave was agreed as well as several free Sundays to preach elsewhere. So all in all I had no real complaints apart from my stipend.

I was rather naive when I said during the negotiations that I would be happy to pay my own expenses, such as petrol expenses. (Interestingly,

Chapter 1

the deacon who was dealing with my contract was happy to accept my recommendation!) However, after careful consideration I changed my mind before the contract was signed and I was very glad I did because the expenses mounted up each quarter.

I know in the olden days it was often the case that the congregation wanted their pastor to live on the poverty line to keep him humble, and so he wouldn't have any spare money to spend on 'worldly pleasures', but we have to ask ourselves, 'Is that attitude right in the sight of God?' Two verses that are important to remember as far as money is concerned: 1 Corinthians 9:14: 'The Lord has commanded that those who preach the gospel should receive their living from the gospel.' And Luke 10:7 where Jesus, in relation to preaching the gospel, says, 'The worker deserves his wages.'

It is also worth considering whether or not your wife should be included in your contract. I will discuss this in more detail later, but suffice it to say now: try to work out how much work your wife will be doing in the church and then consider if it is right for her to be paid for some of what she does. The phrase 'missionary creep' comes to mind. In the first year your wife might only be helping you for a few hours each week. Soon, however, her workload might turn into a full time job!

As can be imagined, it was somewhat galling when I was accused by a member of being paid too much and of wasting the church's money because of my 'high' stipend. Now I know we must not be greedy, but a pastor should be paid a fair living wage and there is no shame in setting out a reasonable stipend request. Pastors, like everyone else, have to live.

When I left the church I recommended to the search committee that the new pastor should be paid according to the FIEC recommendations. Although the church did not go that far, I was pleased to discover that the new man's stipend had been raised by about a third. Churches should be held to account for the way they treat their leaders.

Lessons

- Don't feel guilty about negotiating a fair and reasonable stipend. If in doubt, seek professional advice and even use an intermediary from the FIEC if you think that is necessary. Remember, once you have signed your contract it will be very difficult to change it.

- I made the mistake of trying to have a super-spiritual attitude to my contract as if money didn't matter, thinking, 'Oh well, the Lord will provide.' The way he provides is through the church. So resist the temptation to accept a low stipend that might cause people to praise you for frugality but which leaves your family in need.

- Make sure your contract is as specific as possible about the things you regard as important, such as pension arrangements, holiday allowance, sick pay, Sabbatical, free Sundays and so on. Often church contracts are put together by unqualified but enthusiastic members. So find a professional template to work from or get the FIEC involved so nothing essential is omitted.

- Be prepared that members of the congregation might see your contract, although in my own view it should be a confidential agreement between you and the leaders who signed it. I was disappointed to find out that my elder had shown my contract to a member of the congregation who had been making various complaints against me, which only added fuel to her fire. I know this because she once quoted my contract to me and accused me of breaking it!

Preaching

I am not going to say too much about preaching, partly because it was one of my strengths and on the whole I did not find the mechanics of sermon preparation overly difficult. I have spoken to men who have had to leave

Chapter 1

the pastorate because they struggled to construct three sermons a week. One pastor I spoke to said he took twenty hours to form a sermon and he had to preach three times a week—that's sixty hours a week before he did anything else. No wonder he left the pastorate after only a few years! My successor takes up to fifteen hours per sermon.

For me to take so long preparing a sermon was unworkable, especially as I had two sermons on a Sunday to prepare, plus a mid-week Bible study (all about thirty-five to forty minutes long). On average I would say I spent five to six hours at the most per sermon in preparation (this does not take into consideration 'thinking time' away from my desk). That left me plenty of time each week for other responsibilities. In addition, I would preach at special services such as weddings and funerals and at Easter and Christmas.

Of course the norm today is for many churches to have only one Sunday service and no mid-week Bible study (if that is the case, I wonder what else the pastor gets up to!), or in larger churches to share the preaching load with other men. But if you are thinking of becoming a pastor of a smaller Reformed type church, the probability is that you will be expected to preach three times a week. To change that might be very difficult, so be prepared.

The problem I experienced was not so much with the dynamics of sermon preparation or the actual preaching, but the problem of keeping my sermons fresh and alive, filled with illustrations and interest. It's one thing to prepare a sermon mechanically, it's quite another thing for it to be full of life and power. How can our sermons be 'a demonstration of the Spirit's power'? One way, of course, is for our walk with God to be extremely intimate, alive and refreshing.

There is no question that at times I felt as though I was on a sermon treadmill. As soon as I had finished preaching twice on Sunday, Monday (recovery day) was spent preparing for the Bible study. When that was over, two more sermons had to be ready for Sunday. It became monotonous after a few years. I was also in a church where I did not have suitable men who could regularly preach for me, so if I wanted a Sunday off I would have to import a preacher for the day, which did not always go down well with one of my treasurers because of the expense!

About three years into my ministry, and after I had preached more than four hundred sermons, I hit what I call 'a sermon wall' (a bit like athletes when they 'hit the wall' running). I felt exhausted, not from the physical preparation or delivery, but more from the psychological, mental and emotional stress of having to think continually about sermon preparation. I emailed my fellow leaders to explain the strain I was under and started my letter by saying, 'The job is basically incessant sermon preparation … Every day is sermon preparation—with no let up. Even when I go on holiday, time is spent preparing for when I return because three more sermons are on the near horizon.' Unfortunately I do not remember receiving much practical support as a result of my plea.

Thankfully I did manage to pull myself out of that 'rut' and generally speaking enjoyed sermon preparation and preaching, particularly the Tuesday Bible study. As mentioned before, I did wonder whether the congregation really needed three sermons a week. What good was it doing them having so much food? As someone put it, 'Were they becoming too fat to fly?' If we take extra sermons into account (Easter, Christmas, funerals, weddings, etc.), I was preaching almost every other day during my pastorate.

Lessons

- It's important that in your contract you come to a clear agreement as to how many times you are going to preach each week and how many Sundays off per year you are allowed. One area of confusion that arose was, 'What constitutes a Sunday off?' Was it when I was not preaching but still in the church, perhaps leading the service? Or was it when I was away from the church, either on holiday or preaching elsewhere? It's important for your contract to make that distinction clear. For the first

Chapter 1

half of my ministry it was simply when I was not preaching, regardless of my presence in the church or absence. But then I asked for it to be changed so it meant when I was away from the church. This was partly because of the pastoral issues I had to deal with on a Sunday even when I was not preaching.

- Try to train men who can help with the preaching and leading of services. You may have to persevere with this, especially if a man is not particularly gifted and there are some in the congregation who do not like his preaching. I had some in the congregation who did not want one man preaching on a Sunday because of his 'uneducated' style. My argument was that he needed the practice to improve his style.

- If you are like my elder, who once said to me that it took him 'three days to prepare a sermon', then preaching three times a week will be impossible. Look for a church where the maximum will be once a week. Or, if you dare, tackle the thorny issue of cutting down the number of times you preach, either by using supply preachers, stopping the Sunday evening service or changing the format of the mid-week Bible study. If you try to cut down, some members may well have the attitude: 'Well, what's he being paid for? He's just loafing!'

- I introduced a missionary night once a month on a Tuesday, when we invited a speaker from MAF, Leprosy Mission, Open Doors, etc., to come and tell us about their work. At least it gave me one Tuesday a month when I was not preaching. Later on in my ministry I organised a prayer meeting for the fifth Tuesday in the month.

- Some men have a rule of thumb that we should spend as much time in prayer each week as we do in sermon preparation. I think this is a good rule as it helps to keep us spiritually fresh which will in turn improve our sermons. At all costs we want to avoid sermons that are theologically sound but as dry as dust. William Jay said a 'good sermon should both strike and stick' and that's what we should aim for.

- I would sometimes get quite discouraged over my preaching, thinking it was not accomplishing its purpose. But something I read in Spurgeon's *Lectures to my Students* helped me—it was about a man who was converted eighty-five years after hearing a sermon! Here is the story: John Flavel once cried out at the end of his sermon, 'How can I dismiss you with a blessing for many of you are "Anathema Maranatha", because you love not the Lord Jesus Christ?' A lad of fifteen heard that remarkable utterance and eighty-five years afterwards, sitting under a hedge, the whole scene came vividly before him as if it had been but the day before, and he was wonderfully converted (Spurgeon, *Lectures to my Students*, pp. 392–393).

- There is a proverb that is useful for preachers to remember: 'Though the tongue never tires, the ear does.'

- Here is something else that has helped me. A serious warning was once given to a young Martyn Lloyd-Jones by a much older theologian. In commenting on Lloyd-Jones's sermon, the older man said, 'The great defect of that sermon this afternoon was this: that you were overtaxing your people, you were giving them too much. I will give you a rule; remember it as long as you live: only one in twelve of your congregation is really intelligent. They cannot take it; it is impossible for them to take it. You are only stunning them, and therefore you are not helping them' (Lloyd-Jones, *Preaching and Preachers*, p. 257). I wonder if many pastors take so long preparing their sermons because they are trying to put too much in them.

- I once preached 51 sermons on John 3 and 4, going through those chapters verse by verse. Towards the end of that series my elder came

Chapter 1

to me and said in no uncertain terms, 'I think it's time we moved on!' He was quite right!

- My final piece of advice comes from Robert Murray M'Cheyne, who said, 'I see a man cannot be a faithful minister until he preaches Christ for Christ's sake, until he gives up striving to attract people to himself, and seeks only to attract them to Christ' (Warren Wiersbe, *50 People Every Christian Should Know*, p. 82).

2. The important ones

Let's deal next with the most important people in the church, those men and women who have the most influence and who can make your life an earthly heaven or hell.

My wife
When I started at the church my wife had part-time employment and so could not give much time to church work. I told the leaders that her time was limited, which they accepted without complaint. I also said, when discussing my contract and stipend, that they must not think they are getting 'two for the price of one'; that is, they are not employing me, then expecting my wife to work many hours for the church for free. Quite a few pastors I know wisely get their wives to be employed by the church so that this 'two for one' situation cannot arise. As time passes by, it is inevitable that our wives will become more and more involved.

This was certainly what I experienced. After about a year of my pastorate it became obvious that I needed my wife's help in many ways, so she gave up her part-time job to assist me, which of course reduced our income. Although she ended up giving many hours a week to church work, she was never paid a penny for what she did. We never asked for any nor was any offered to us. As I never visited a lady member without my wife, she would come visiting with me every day, sometimes for hours at a time. She ran the ladies' group, sorted out the data projection each week, helped to type out the church hymns, catalogued my sermon illustrations, assisted with catering and flowers … and so the list goes on. She ended up being the church administrator and my personal secretary, and worked many more hours than she had done at her part-time job. And I must say she never complained. One of the reasons for such heavy involvement was

Chapter 2

because there were few others in the church who were either willing or able to do this work.

I must say at this point that at no time did my wife receive any criticism from the church. Quite often the pastor's wife is a source of irritation to some members. This might be partly due to the wife's strong character, or maybe she speaks out of turn, which annoys some, but I was grateful that I never heard anyone speak detrimentally about my wife. Sometimes, when members came to complain about me, they would specifically say that their comments did not refer to my wife. She always got away with it!

Lessons

- Your relationship with your wife is the most important in the church. Be alert that the devil and even some church members will try to test that relationship. Keep short accounts with each other and be open and honest at all times.

- Think long and hard about the role of your wife before you start your pastorate. Will she be needed to work for the church? Are there many others who could help out? Should she be given a part-time contract by the church, especially if she has to give up paid employment to assist? Try to make the distinction between what she does as a member and duties that will require remuneration. Beware, too, that some churches will never countenance paying the pastor's wife. It's a kind of principle they hold.

- While it is true that many members give up their time to run a ministry in the church (free of charge) and rightly so, just think about the time your wife is spending probably doing multiple tasks. It's one thing running a single ministry for two or three hours a fortnight, it's quite another spending three hours a day, every day, helping the pastor with his work load. Unfortunately, some churches take advantage of a pastor's wife in a way that secular employers would never do.

- Of course, look carefully at the church's financial situation. Is the church able to afford to pay your wife? While you do not want to put unnecessary strain on the church's finances, a worker is worth her wages.

- Towards the close of Lloyd-Jones's life, Iain Murray asked him what kind of woman he thought a minister's wife should be. He replied, 'What she needs above everything is wisdom, so that she does not create problems. And another thing is this, she should never have a special friend in the church. That is very important. Otherwise it will create division and jealousy. Her main business is to look after her husband—relieve him of worries about the home, about food, as far as she can about financial matters and, very important, not to keep on feeding him with the tittle tattle of the gossip of the church. She is to protect him and to help him' (Iain Murray, *The Fight of Faith*, p. 762). In other words, it is more important for the wife to look after her husband than to look after the church.

- John Watson, in his *The Cure of Souls*, says a good wife 'advises her husband on every important matter, and often restrains him from hasty speech ... receives him weary, discouraged, irritable, and sends him out again strong, hopeful, sweet-tempered' (pp. 235–6). I am so thankful to God that my wife was always on my side and never caused me any trouble in the church.

The predecessor

It's an interesting question as to what your predecessor should do, especially if he is retiring and not moving on to pastor another church. Should he stay in the church or should he leave? I know one pastor who

Chapter 2

asked his predecessor to leave for a year. Then when that year was up he felt it was not long enough so he asked him to stay away for another year. He then returned and it worked quite well. I know another man who said the former pastor could stay but he was not allowed to attend any of the members' meetings and so had no influence on any decisions the church made. In this case there was no problem as the retired pastor was out preaching at other churches most weeks, so was rarely around. The congregation could see that he had an itinerant ministry and their allegiance was towards the new man.

I recently spoke to a pastor who resigned from his church after just a few years. When I asked why, one of the reasons he cited was that the former pastor was the only other elder and he did not want anything in the church to change from his time as leader. He was effectively trying to run the church from his new position as the second elder, which of course was a recipe for disaster.

One thing I'll say to start with is that if a man has been leading a church for several years or longer and stays in that church when a new pastor comes, it is very difficult for him not to give his opinion or to 'interfere' with how the church is run. For him just to keep quiet and to turn a blind eye to everything that is going on or changing is tough. He has led the church for years, it was his 'baby', so it is understandable that he finds it hard to let go, especially if he has not gone on to another ministry.

In my case the previous pastor was urged by some of his friends in the church to leave, but his response was, 'Where could I go?' Actually in our area there were many churches of every size and type from which to choose. He kindly asked my permission to stay. I was in a bit of a quandary. I knew it wasn't ideal for him to stay, but he was a gracious and gentle man. I reasoned that he probably wouldn't be around much because he would be preaching most weeks in other churches. He promised not to interfere and I reasoned that as the numbers in the church were already small, for him and his wife to leave along with their daughter, a big hole would be left. So I allowed him to stay. This was a mistake.

It was not a mistake because he was demanding or aggressive or didn't want things to change. On the contrary, for the first couple of years he was a great encouragement, writing me little notes of appreciation and appearing to offer me his full support. He also took on the role as treasurer when the previous treasurer resigned, a much needed role to be filled. This I think was also a mistake, because he could see exactly what my expenses were and inevitably compared them to his own expenses when he was the pastor.

So what was the problem? Firstly, he was not away most weeks preaching. In fact, he only preached away from the church about once a year. So he was at every meeting—at both services on the Sunday, at every prayer meeting and members' meeting, at every special event. Now of course that's what you want from your members, commitment! But it was not what I had expected. He also attended ministers' fraternals, which made it difficult for me to be open about any problems in my church as I had a member of that church sitting right by me.

He also had a loyal group in the church, who had imbibed his ways and were quite rigid about spiritual things, and tended to side with him if there was any difference of opinion. So unwittingly, as far as he was concerned, we had two groups, one who supported the old pastor and his rather antiquated ways, and those who supported the new, who wanted to modernise the church in a few areas. This obviously created tension.

Thirdly, as the months went by he could not help trying to influence the decisions of the church. In other words, he interfered in a way that he had promised not to. To begin with it was in minor ways. Fairly early on in my ministry Christmas Day was on a Sunday. I was wondering whether to have just one service on that day so people could spend time with their families. He came up to me and wagged his finger at me and said sternly: 'two services'. This was not a request but a demand. It put me in an awkward position, because I didn't want to go against his desire, but I also had others to think about. In the end we had two services and I was surprised at how many came to the evening service, although admittedly

Chapter 2

some came from other churches who were not having an evening service. We actually had family from abroad staying with us for the day and they graciously came along in the evening, although they were a bit surprised we were having a service.

Perhaps a bigger interference was when I was thinking about having someone alongside me to help with some of the responsibilities. I was toying with the idea of having a Bible College student on placement and I shared this idea with the members. My predecessor immediately piped up and said he had had four such placements in his time and they had all been a failure. In other words, it was a waste of time pursuing this idea. (I subsequently heard from another member that things didn't work well with the placements partly because they were not allowed to do anything in the church and became frustrated and bored.) Such a comment made it very difficult for me to pursue a Bible College student because it would never have been passed by the membership. I felt like saying to him, 'Well, you had four attempts, let me have one!'

When we were thinking of putting aside hymn books for data projection, I called him up to have a chat about it to get his opinion. He seemed to have no problem with it. When we eventually changed to data projection, I was surprised to see him and his wife and daughter refuse to put down the hymn book during the hymns. All three of them held their books high in the air in order to hide the data projection screen from their view. In doing so they made a clear statement to the rest of the church.

Although I was initially pleased when he said he would be the treasurer, I was also rather apprehensive. He saw my stipend and all my expenses and although he never said anything to me directly and was only supportive in his financial reports to the membership, I did hear from another member that he had made various criticisms about my expenses. This was out of character, because he generally kept his thoughts about money to himself and was a private man. His intention was certainly not to stir up trouble for me.

I found it difficult to make any significant changes in the church in case he took it personally as a criticism of how he used to do things. His presence made it harder to make a clean break with the past and somewhat tied my hands in a way that he did not intend. I also felt uncomfortable when things went really well in the church and new people were attending, because I thought he might be a little envious in case things had not gone so well during his pastorate. When people started to leave, I thought he might be thinking, 'This never happened in my day.' To be honest, I'm sure these feelings were down to my own silly sensitivities, but they would not have occurred if he had not been present in the church.

In allowing him to stay I had not thought too much about his wife, who was a much more outspoken individual. She was not afraid of speaking her mind. Once she caused a pastoral issue when she strongly criticised an old lady in the church who wanted to sell some of her home-made jam in the church hall (to members and others) on a weekday, sending the proceeds to one of our missionaries. My predecessor's wife came charging up to me when she heard about what was going to happen and said, 'Why are we having a jumble sale in the church and turning it into a bazaar?' This upset the old lady and I had a job to reassure her. She then didn't feel able to sell her jam on the church premises.

One issue that was more difficult to resolve, because it involved the whole membership, was when some of the hymns I had introduced into the church were criticised by a few in a members' meeting for being too 'modern'. After a while the ex-pastor's wife cried out, 'All the new hymns are just about "me". They all say I, I, I.' By this time in the discussion I felt a bit tense and had to stop myself from giving my opinion in too forceful a manner. My opinion was threefold: one, all the new hymns are not filled with 'I, I, I'. That statement was simply incorrect. Second, what's wrong with having 'I' in a hymn? Many of the old classics have 'I' in them, 'Just as I am', 'Amazing Grace' to name just two. Third, had she never read the Psalms, the hymnbook of Israel? It is full of 'I' and many of the psalms are very personal.

Chapter 2

After this particular meeting I had various fallouts to resolve. I did wonder about my wisdom in allowing such an open discussion, but I had been pressurized by one of my deacons to allow it. He thought it would clear the air if people were allowed to 'get things off their chest'. My elder thought I had handled the meeting 'brilliantly', but I was not so sure. I also realised that he was pleased because his 'favourite' in the church had been allowed to voice her opinion (more on that later). Did the meeting help? Unfortunately it made things worse and I think the church never fully recovered.

After about four years I noticed a slight change in the former pastor's attitude towards me. He never said anything to me directly, but the encouraging notes and comments stopped. His wife started to lose concentration during my preaching and made it obvious she was not listening. Then suddenly out of the blue they wanted to talk with me after a Tuesday meeting. I knew what they were going to say because the previous evening their daughter and her new husband came to me and said they were leaving the church, because, in their words, 'they didn't want to be a divisive influence'. So I was prepared. Sure enough, after a short statement that they had felt uncomfortable for a while, they resigned their membership with immediate effect. They handed me a courteous 'thank you' letter and walked out of the church, never again to return under my pastorate. I was disappointed they had never discussed any problems with me or explained their reasons for leaving. To this day I have no idea why they left.

All sorts of rumours started to circulate. Their departure caused problems among his group of supporters, who blamed me for driving them out. One member told me to chase after them and bring them back, while accusing me of 'scattering the sheep' like an Old Testament false prophet. I don't think his supporters ever forgave me.

Lessons

- May I say first of all that it's important to be gracious and patient towards your predecessor. He may well be struggling with retirement and with a hands off approach. After so many years in charge, when everyone was looking to him for a lead, it comes as a shock to many men to find that they are now just 'pew warmers' and the congregation they loved and served is now following another man.

- The most obvious lesson must be to ask the previous pastor to leave when you take over. My predecessor was the most gracious man imaginable, but his presence caused difficulties, many of which were not his fault. When he finally left after about four years that caused further problems. If he had left the church on my arrival, I'm sure the congregation would have understood, but leaving when he did made many jump to the wrong conclusions. Personally I can see little benefit if he stays.

- If you do want him to stay for whatever reason, then consider his wife, children, and supporters in the church. Think about his temperament, his theology, his likes and dislikes. Will he be able to submit to your leadership, preaching, personality, your way of doing things without a murmur? How will he respond if you close a ministry he had started or implement something that is the complete opposite of what he would have done?

- His presence alone in the church can be enough to force people to take sides, to stick with the old way rather than follow the new.

- If he stays, I would keep a close dialogue with him so that you both understand each other. You could remind him and his wife not to publicly oppose you if you are wanting to implement something about which he would disapprove or have reservations. I think I failed to consult him enough, to include him. I should have treated him more as a friend and less as a threat.

Chapter 2

- A numerically strong family in the church can be a great blessing but also a problem that needs to be handled wisely. Sometimes family loyalties come before church loyalties. If one family makes up too high a percentage of the membership, it can become a power struggle between the leadership and the family.

- It is a good idea to have in your own mind the Biblical reasons for leaving a church. Should a member of your congregation leave because they do not like some of the hymns or because a fellow member irritates them? When are you justified in leaving a church and when are you guilty of schism? Search the Scriptures to find your answers.

- Should you chase after members who have left, in a bid to convince them to return? It is tricky to have a hard and fast rule for every resignation. Some might be 'blessed subtractions', others might be worth the time and effort it takes to convince them to stay. The reason for their resignation might be easy to resolve, so there are times when a conversation is worthwhile. I only attempted it once, and failed.

Elders and deacons

Choosing the right elders and deacons to work alongside you is vital. A good leadership team can be fantastic and bring great glory to God in their unity, loyalty and hard work. A divisive leadership can destroy the church. It is better to have no leadership team at all than a bad one. The problem is that when you go to a new church the leadership is usually already in place and it is difficult to get rid of men who do not fit in with your plans. You can't exactly sack them all and start again from scratch! Would they all resign so they could be re-elected on your recommendation? I doubt it. It would be better if you could start with a clean slate and choose men as you go along, but that is rarely possible.

When I arrived at my church there were five deacons and no elders, although a couple of deacons were really elders in all but name because of the work they were doing. Not long after my initial appointment one of the deacons left. There had been disagreement and misunderstanding between him and the other deacons before I arrived, partly over my desire for a probationary period. This deacon thought I should be one hundred percent committed to the church from the start. In many ways I understood his point of view. He also came to me and told me that, while he enjoyed my preaching, in his opinion 'I was not a pastor', a somewhat hasty judgement as I had only been at the church a short while; but it was not a good start. After he and his wife left there were no further issues along those lines.

Sadly, a second deacon died soon after I arrived. He was a lovely, gracious man and was sorely missed by us all. That left three deacons and me. I was happy with that and I looked at the three men closely to see if one of them could become an elder. I also considered men from the congregation, but there did not seem to be anyone with the necessary gifting. I wanted an elder as it was important for me to have someone I could confide in and who would stand with me both publicly and privately.

Perhaps I should say now that I was generally happy with these three men. Although they were elderly and two of them did not have many years in front of them, they did what they could and helped me to understand the history of the church. The one area they fell down on was their lack of public support of me over various decisions that we had made. We always made the decisions together, came to an agreement and then presented them to the church. That was all fine as long as everyone was happy with our decisions and proposals. However, if there was any opposition, the three men would leave me to do all the explaining and convincing, and rarely say anything publicly in support of the proposal we had all agreed. At times this gave the impression that they were not happy with what was being put to the church. I think they just wanted a peaceful life, as we all do.

Here is one example. We all agreed to go ahead with data projection in the hope of phasing out hymn books. In fact, we were all enthusiastic about the change. Two women in the church were not! They met with

Chapter 2

all four of us and told us rather aggressively their objections to what we were planning. (We may talk about this later in more detail.) Suffice it to say here that I noticed that the other three men did not say a single word during the whole encounter. Their silence (and nodding) gave the impression that this was solely my idea and they were going along with it reluctantly. It would have been much better if they had pinned their colours to the mast and supported openly what we had agreed in private. It also made me feel slightly concerned that they might not fully support me if others complained about me when I was not present. In time this suspicion proved to be correct, as we shall see.

It is important to choose men for leadership who will be prepared to support you in public: men who will fight for you, men who will stand by you when the chips are down, through thick and thin, men who will not crumble at the first sign of opposition, and who will be strong enough to resist members of the congregation who are out to cause trouble.

Nevertheless, from these three men I chose an elder and I was pleased with my choice. He was a man well respected within the congregation, with many years of pastoral experience. I felt he could advise me, and he was happy to spend quality time with me in prayer. We became good friends. The only slight downsides were that he lived about a forty-five minute drive away, which meant it was not practical to meet too often; he was, to use his own expression, 'allergic to the telephone', so we did not speak on the phone very much. He was hard of hearing without his aid, so when I did phone he always had it on loudspeaker and so his wife heard everything I said and invariably would answer before my elder, who would then just repeat what she had said. This became rather irritating, so I asked him to take the phone into another room when I called. I was never sure if he did or whether his wife just whispered her replies so that I could not hear. He also found it difficult to write emails (being dyslexic), and so invariably his wife wrote them for him.

The only other negative was his desire to criticise members of the congregation. This started almost as soon as he became my elder. He sometimes went back years in his criticisms. I found that what he said was colouring my own views of the members, and so I had to tell him to stop and to be more positive so that he wasn't influencing me the wrong way. What happened before my arrival at the church did not really concern me unless it was in some way affecting the present situation.

These were only minor irritants. He was a godly man who often gave me sound counsel. Because of his age he did not do as much as I would have liked in the church, but he was certainly a great help. My wife and I had some precious times of prayer with him and his wife and for the first four or five years we got on well with a mutual respect in our relationship and a close friendship. There are many positive things I could mention about him, but as my focus is on what goes wrong in the pastorate I shall resist.

The turning point came when he decided to resign from the eldership because of his age. I was sorry about his decision. As there was no one else who could take his place at that point, I asked him to reconsider, to stay on for another year in a reduced capacity. To this he agreed. His new role was less practical, but he was there when I needed to chat. I was happy with that.

One of the problems that arose was because of a close relationship he had with a member of the congregation (the 'favourite' mentioned earlier). They had been friends for years when, totally unbeknown to me, she started to call him up to complain about me and to make various accusations against me (this happened during his 'semi-retirement' year). Instead of showing his support to me, he gave her a sympathetic ear, so much so that she started to call him with her complaints most nights. She then wrote out a 'ream' of complaints against me and handed them to him. Interestingly, he never told me or challenged me about a single accusation that she had lodged against me, and did not even bother to read all her written accusations himself. I found all this out later.

As I now look back I can see that most things he said, did or wrote to me during his final eldership year had been coloured by what she had said. For instance, in one of our meetings together he criticised me and said

Chapter 2

there was someone in the congregation who had told him that 'unless the pastor goes, I go'. Well, I knew immediately that he was talking about his 'friend'. This woman then wrote me a poisoned letter, which she also gave to all the leaders. The other deacons were shocked by it and one of them wrote a lengthy reply in which he called the letter 'vindictive'. My elder was unconcerned about what his friend had written to me, but he went to great lengths to compel my deacon to apologise for using the word 'vindictive' in his reply because it had been upsetting to his friend.

Sadly, towards the end of my time at the church our relationship completely broke down. I gave the church six months written notice of my resignation and was happy to help set up a search committee to look for a new pastor. The elder, who was now no longer an elder, emailed me the day after my resignation and offered to lead the search committee. His immediate response and enthusiasm to do so was not missed by my deacons! He wanted to get the congregation's support, so he asked if he could mention it to the congregation the following Sunday. I agreed.

When the Sunday arrived I let him speak from the pulpit. Out of the blue he declared that he not only wanted to lead the search committee but wanted to be re-elected as an elder as well. This was the first I'd heard about his desire to be an elder again. Previously he'd told me he did not want to be an elder again, which is why he had resigned some time ago. After the service I took him to one side and told him he was wrong to put himself forward as an elder without any consultation with the church officers. I was still the pastor. He agreed that it was 'probably wrong'. Our chat was amicable and I thought that was that.

The next Sunday he called me into a side room to say that he no longer wanted to head up the search committee. Meanwhile his wife was giving all the members of the church a misleading letter about me (I never received a copy of the letter but members showed me their copies). As to the contents of the letter, the reaction of some of the members will give you an idea. They said it was 'shocking', 'cruel', 'nasty', 'it finished me off'. It caused great distress in the church.

Why am I dragging all this up now? Just to warn you about the importance of choosing a good elder and guarding your relationship with him. If your relationship with your elder turns sour, it can have devastating consequences for the church and for you personally.

Lessons

- Choose your elders and deacons carefully. Not only should they fulfil the Biblical requirements for leadership (1 Timothy 3; Titus 1), but you must be confident they fit in well with your personality and desires for the church. They must be men who are prepared to stand by you even when you are under fire. A fair weather leader is no good at all.

- Try to choose men who are not too old, men with energy and vision, rather than men who are on their last legs and who are looking to escape the responsibility. This is easier said than done. In a small church you often don't have many men (if any) who meet the qualifications.

- If an elder wants to resign for legitimate reasons, think very carefully before you try to persuade him to stay on. Remember it is better for you to have no elder than to have a reluctant one.

- Tell your leaders not to have favourites within the church. It caused tremendous heartache for me. If we have favourites, we are not able to deal with people and situations impartially and objectively. Having favourites or particularly close friends can cause split loyalties when difficulties arise, as they surely will. As someone has said, 'A man who wants to conduct the orchestra must turn his back on the crowd.'

- Be careful about giving a sympathetic ear to a complaining member, especially if the complaint is about one of your fellow leaders and appears unjustified. The more you sympathise, the more they will return

Chapter 2

with another complaint. Remember a 'gossip separates close friends' (Proverbs 16:28).

- It is a serious matter for an accusation to be levelled against an elder. It is vital that you abide by the 'two or three witnesses' rule (2 Corinthians 13:1; 1 Timothy 5:19). Be alert to the tactics of the devil who is always wanting to bring division and suspicion among the leadership of the church.

- When trust breaks down it's very hard to restore it. So nip things in the bud. My elder had an opportunity to resolve things with me but refused.

- Betrayal is a strong word, but that is how I felt. Psalm 55:12–14 was real for me: 'If an enemy were insulting me, I could endure it; if a foe were raising himself against me, I could hide from him. But it is you, a man like myself, my companion, my close friend, with whom I once enjoyed sweet fellowship as we walked with the throng at the house of God.'

- Spurgeon wisely said, 'If you resist Satan, he will fly from you; if you resist one of your deacons, he will fly at you.'

- Consider training men for particular roles, although the words of D. L. Moody are worth contemplating, 'It is better to train ten men than to do the work of ten men, but it's harder.'

- Work hard on your relationship with your leaders. Support them, pray for them, be open with them. Always treat them with respect. They need your help almost as much as you need their help. Remember if your relationship with them deteriorates, it will have a negative impact on the church sooner or later and God will not be glorified by it.

The treasurer

The treasurer has an extremely important position, partly because it involves money. Money can be a divisive and controversial topic, especially when it comes to spending it! So a treasurer must be chosen with the utmost care. The individual must obviously have the necessary skills, but they do not have to be an elder or deacon.

During my time I had four different treasurers. Three of them were fine and didn't cause any difficulties within the church. They conducted their duties with integrity and care, and gave an honest and straightforward account at the members' meetings. While they had slightly different methods of working, the 'books' were always kept in good order. My final treasurer was the best in my opinion. She was supportive and generous, a good communicator, and she did not mind spending money.

Unfortunately I had one treasurer who was difficult beyond words. When the previous treasurer resigned, there was really only one person in the church who could do the job from a mathematical point of view. This is one of the difficulties in a small church—you do not get much of a choice sometimes. You do not get three or four different people applying for the post where you can choose the most suitable. It is often a choice between one person and nobody. And of course you cannot be your own treasurer!

What I didn't know at the time was the person we chose was strongly opposed to me. I had not noticed any obvious difficulty before the appointment, or else I would not have accepted her into this important position. But it soon became apparent that she had an axe to grind, which she was prepared to do in a very public fashion. So when she came to give her first financial report before the members, she made the most of her opportunity. She directly criticised my stipend, criticised the money the church had spent (which of course was principally my responsibility), criticised the proposed increase of 3% to my stipend. She presented bar charts that showed how much money I was taking out of the church (this included my stipend and expenses). On to my particular bar of the chart, which was much higher than all the other bars, she added what the church

Chapter 2

paid supply preachers and other expenses that were not directly mine. And so I could go on. This made it look as though I was being paid a fortune and unnecessarily spending all the money in the church, which was far from the truth.

I must admit I sat in the meeting shell shocked. Shocked because I had not expected such a personal public attack, and shocked because of how the accounts had been twisted to paint the pastor in a bad light. My immediate reaction was to make light of it in front of the other members, but my wife and I were inwardly furious. Now what should I do in such a situation? With hindsight that should have been the last time she ever gave a report. But who else could do the job? Sadly things deteriorated from that point. I did try to speak to her, but it became so personal and hurtful that I shied away. What made things more difficult was the fact that she was my elder's 'favourite' mentioned above.

There is no point going into the long list of attacks that she made on me, very few to my face. These were attacks I heard about from others. After what seemed an interminably long time she resigned from her position with a nasty letter that she sent to the whole leadership team. Soon afterwards she left the church. Thankfully by that time the Lord had raised up another member who was ready and willing to take over and she did a superb job.

I didn't really detect this at the time, but since then I have looked back and analysed what happened, I see quite clearly the hand of Satan in many of these events. This person was being used by him to create as much trouble as possible for the church and its pastor. One reason I mention this is because there was an unreasonableness about her actions. She would not listen to reason or any explanation that I gave in answer to her accusations. Even one of her supporters called her 'irrational'. And some of the things she did were unconscionable. Satan is unreasonable. He is not ready to listen to sound arguments. He has no conscience to bother him or make him think. He is only interested in attacking God's people and will do all he can to destroy us.

I honestly feel that Satan is becoming the forgotten foe in the evangelical church. So when something goes wrong, we tend to blame everyone but him. I admit that during these troubles I was mostly blind to the activities of the devil. Part of the reason for such ignorance is because Satan is hard to spot. He looks like an angel of light. He is a master at disguise and camouflage. His voice sounds like the voice of God. His 'suggestions' appear to be Biblical. That is why we need to be alert and watchful.

Not too long ago my wife and I went to a RSPB reserve. As we were sitting in one of the hides a fellow bird watcher pointed into the distance and said, 'Look, a snipe!' I looked and looked with my naked eye (we did not have binoculars) but couldn't see anything. The man then kindly said, 'Here, look through my telescope.' Amazingly the snipe became clearly visible. Knowing exactly where he was I again looked with my naked eye, but I still could not spot it. It was so well camouflaged against the reeds. I say again, Satan is hard to spot. Apparently snipes fly in a zigzag fashion making them hard to shoot. If you are a marksman, you will be able to shoot them and will be called a 'sniper'. Satan is hard to shoot. He is all over the place. One minute here, the next over there. That is why we must be self-controlled and alert, and never forget the kind of foe we are fighting.

The only other point I shall make about my treasurer is that she was what I call a 'recruiter'. She tried hard to recruit others to support her against me, to enlist other members to join her party. She was not content to fight alone. This kind of attitude can divide a church and make it difficult for the pastor to work effectively.

Lessons

- Money can be a divisive topic and so can your stipend. R. T. Kendall said in the *Evangelical Times* how 'as a young pastor the church decided that generally speaking my salary would be the average of the other elders' salaries from their secular employment. I was neither richer nor poorer. It was a good decision and God blessed the church.' For me, I only had one elder and he was retired, but Kendall's comment is a good place to start.

- Be as transparent about money as possible. I itemised everything I spent and kept all receipts.

- It is important that you choose a treasurer who has the same, or similar, philosophy as you about money. Some treasurers never want to spend a penny and are far too frugal. This can halt progress in the church and cause you to fight over every pound you want to spend. Some are too extravagant and fall back on 'the Lord will provide' mantra. Somewhere in between these two extremes is the most helpful. In all your thoughts about money, remember this saying, 'Money will buy a fine dog, but only love will make him wag his tail.'

- Have a detailed conversation with your prospective treasurer before you appoint him (or her) to be the treasurer. This will give you the opportunity to see if he is the right fit for you and the church and will help to avoid any future misunderstanding. Unfortunately I did not speak beforehand to my treasurer. If I had done so, it might have saved a mountain of problems.

- Keep the channels of communication open between yourself and the treasurer, so both parties know what is going on with the financial side of the church. I could have been better at communication with all my treasurers about what the church was proposing to spend.

- As a shepherd, know the condition of your sheep well, so you can detect problems and sort out the situation before it escalates (Proverbs 27:23-27). This knowledge will also prevent you from making bad appointments.

- Do not be surprised if there are people in your church who cause trouble. We are all sinners so it is bound to happen at some point.

- Beware of becoming cynical about certain members, especially those who are always causing you difficulties. Cynicism is not a godly attitude and needs to be confessed to the Lord.

- Remember that when there is serious conflict in the church, it will be discovered or felt by the other members. They might not know exactly what is going on, but they will be able to detect that something is wrong. Besides, will God continue to bless where there is serious animosity and discord within the church family? (Psalm 133).

- Never forget that we do not fight against flesh and blood but against the evil powers of darkness (Ephesians 6:12). Watch and pray, and 'be strong in the Lord and in his mighty power' (Ephesians 6:10).

- In difficult situations, it is often only our walk with God that we can fall back on. Keep close to Jesus. Pour out your heart to him. He knows exactly what is going on. He knows every motive and word spoken in secret. He understands you fully. You can trust him absolutely.

Volunteers

Having come from a working environment where we only had the odd volunteer and everyone else was on the payroll, it took a while to adjust to volunteers, who of course can come and go as they like. In the workplace everyone has their own position and area of responsibility. There are rules that govern timekeeping, behaviour, targets, etc., and if these rules are broken there are various sanctions that are in place.

With volunteers it is completely different. If they can't or don't want to turn up on a particular day, you just have to get on without them. If they decide to walk away from their position, they don't necessarily have

Chapter 2

to give any notice. Because they often work hard and do not receive any monetary reward, they can be more sensitive than ordinary workers. A cross word here, an impatient spirit there, or insisting on their doing something they don't want to do, means you can end up losing a fine helper. In the workplace you can insist on certain things, but 'laying down the law' is more difficult with volunteers.

In a small church, where the pastor is the only paid worker, it is impossible for the church to run without volunteers. They are invaluable, whether they are stewards, musicians, leaders, Sunday school workers, caterers, cleaners, or whatever—the church cannot function without them. That is why it is imperative for the pastor to nurture, encourage, cajole, train—do whatever it takes—to keep and stand by good volunteers.

One area where I didn't quite get it right was in the area of the Sunday school. We had a small Sunday school run by a few faithful workers. I noticed that the leaders did not sing with the children, so I suggested it would be great if the children were taught a few simple songs that they could go home singing. I had someone ready to play the piano to help them. I encountered immediate opposition. 'If I spend time singing with the children, I won't be able to get through all my material in the time.' 'I'm no good at singing.' 'I don't know any children's songs.' It was obvious my suggestion did not go down well, but I tried to press my case for the good of the children, but without being too insistent, thinking, 'If I push too hard, the leaders will walk away and there is no one else who could take the Sunday school.' So in the end I gave up and left them to run it in the way that seemed best to them.

Sadly, after a number of years the Sunday school petered out, although the leaders were always ready in case any children turned up. So then I had to wrestle with the question: how do you start a Sunday school from scratch? This I found very difficult. A fellow pastor, whose church was similar to mine, overcame the problem by having seven children of his own, who made up the Sunday school! Now is that cheating? At least it's a start, but I was far too old to go down that route. My problem was that whenever a family came to the church and saw there was no Sunday school for their children, they never returned, much to everyone's disappointment. I thought about starting a mums and toddlers group, but I needed more volunteers. I had also heard from other pastors that the mums came to the midweek group but did not bring their children to the church on Sundays, so I dropped the idea. Unfortunately, I never managed to restart the Sunday school.

Lessons

- Volunteers must be chosen carefully. A good volunteer is invaluable, but a bad one can be far more trouble than they are worth. Sherry Anderson is right when she says, 'Volunteers don't get paid, not because they're worthless, but because they're priceless.'

- Treat volunteers with great respect. They are giving up their time and energy to work for God in the church and that should not be taken for granted.

- Volunteers tend to need a few more 'thank yous' than paid workers. It is often the only reward they get. So treat them gently and show your appreciation for them on as many occasions as possible.

- One of the keys is to put the right volunteer into the right role, making the most of their gifts and expertise. Never try to fit a round peg in a square hole, however desperate you are to fill a particular position.

3. Treading on eggshells

I have called this section 'treading on eggshells' because I found that the issues listed below were the most sensitive and in many ways the most difficult to deal with wisely. This was partly because a vocal minority wanted to have their say and get their way. Often they were not willing to compromise or to find any middle ground for the sake of peace. This inevitably led to difficulties.

Music

Interestingly, before I started at the church someone said to me that the three most troublesome areas of church life were music, flowers and catering. Thankfully we had no problems with flowers or catering and I only have happy memories of how the ladies (mostly) arranged the flowers and were always so willing to prepare a 'feast' for special occasions. However, I find it sad that I have to put music under the heading of 'difficult areas', but unfortunately that is what it became—a difficult and controversial area in my church.

This was true partly because there were so many different hymns and songs to choose from and partly because there was such a variety of musical tastes represented. Everyone had their own personal preferences, their 'heart music', as someone described it. When I arrived there was an organ and a piano and the hymns that were sung were old and traditional. I tried, with limited success, to introduce some more modern hymns. Most of the congregation enjoyed them, but a number were upset that we were, in their view, introducing 'worldly' hymns, and they refused to sing them. By the way, the kind of hymns we are talking about were mainly written by Keith Getty and Stuart Townend—in other words, nothing too radical but more modern.

One of the problems we encountered was down to the fact that the musicians were elderly and had been used to playing only old traditional hymns; they found it difficult to play the new hymns with their different musical style. Some of the new music was syncopated and they struggled to adjust to the timing. This was understandable, so I tried to pick those modern hymns that were easier for them to play.

Our main musician, who was the only one who could play the organ, was very talented, but 'for conscience sake' refused to play any hymn of which she did not approve. I was given a list of about 60 or 70 hymns that were on her forbidden list and which I had to avoid choosing. One of the more bizarre reasons she gave was that some of the hymns/songs were too short and therefore not acceptable to God in worship! Although her theology was more than a little dubious I accepted her wishes, partly because she led the musicians, and partly because if I had tried to compel her to play certain hymns, she probably would have left the church and taken her daughter with her, who was also part of the music team. That would have left me without any real musicians in the congregation, apart from a couple of ladies who occasionally played but who were not particularly gifted. She was in a position of strength to get her own way. So I felt trapped and forced into a decision I did not really want to take. I often thought of that joke which asks: 'What's the difference between an organist and terrorist?' The answer: 'You can negotiate with a terrorist.' At times I really wanted to crack it to our organist, but didn't dare. The scary thing is I think there is some truth in the joke!

I remember once talking to an elderly lady who was passionate about the 'old hymns'. I told her I was just trying to introduce a few modern hymns that the younger generation could relate to and that we didn't want to be too old fashioned. Her immediate response was, 'Well, God is old-fashioned!' Now what do you say to that?

When I was in the midst of this 'hymn controversy' I went on holiday with my wife to Amsterdam. While we were there we went to the Bible museum and I could not help chuckling to myself when I read

Chapter 3

the following, which shows that 'hymn hatred' is not just a modern phenomenon:

'In 1807 evangelical hymns are adopted in the Reformed church. The text of these hymns is taken from the New Testament. The hymns are intended as songs of praise to Christ and the church and are sung during the worship service in addition to the Old Testament psalms. Some of the orthodox members of the church refuse to sing the hymns. The hymn question arouses very heated emotions throughout the nineteenth century. The Rev. Schouten is a passionate supporter of the singing of the evangelical hymns. He describes the "hymn hatred" of his contemporaries as "an absurd fervour to condemn everything that might be called new" and regards it as a denial of Christ.'

When I read this I thought about those words in Ecclesiastes: 'What has been will be again, what has been done will be done again; there is nothing new under the sun' (Ecclesiastes 1:9).

So my attempts to make things a little more modern only partially got off the ground, but it was a battle. I felt my efforts were resented by some, who thought it was their remit to keep Isaac Watts and Charles Wesley at the top of every agenda. Funnily enough, I read about a church who only wanted to sing the hymns of Isaac Watts but only if they all had the same tune!

Lessons

- I really did feel as though the music in the church was like treading on eggshells, because it was impossible to please everyone. Those who had strong views were not slow in coming forward. Some members simply would not sing a hymn they found 'theologically unacceptable'. So it was a genuine challenge to bring everyone together musically.

- There is an expression that used to be heard frequently in Wales to do with congregational singing, and it meant 'the demon of singing'. 'What it meant was that this question of singing caused more quarrelling and divisions in churches than practically anything else, that singing gave the devil more frequent opportunities of hindering and disrupting the work than any other activity in church life' (Martyn Lloyd-Jones, *Preaching and Preachers*, pp. 266–267). That is why we must tread softly. Music is a sensitive area. Try to encourage, cajole, reason with your members rather than using a more aggressive or forthright approach.

- An important question that needs to be asked is: who chooses the hymns for the Sunday services? Is it the musicians, the service leaders, the pastor or the congregation? If possible, I think you should try to get a harmonious agreement among all parties. It is not for any one group (the pastor included) to impose their likes and dislikes on everyone else. Ideally the old and the young should defer to each other.

- In hindsight, I think I should have been more committed in trying to persuade my organist to play the hymns she did not want to play, rather than just passively accepting her refusal (although I did have a number of conversations with her). This would have risked losing her, but it was a risk I should have taken. If she had left the church, I could have used background music for the singing, as I know other churches do if they do not have any musicians willing or able to play.

- Whenever you make any changes in a church, it is vital that a proper explanation be given as to why the changes are being made, to try to persuade the congregation that what you are doing is best for the church as a whole. Then graciously stick to your principles and do not let any individual or group in the church browbeat you into submitting to their demands.

- Remember, too, that Christians relate to their 'heart music', which may be the music they were brought up on or music from when they were first converted. For some it is the old hymns, for others it's choruses from the 1970s, for others it's songs written by their favourite musician. All this has to be taken into consideration when planning the musical direction of the church.

- The questions we need to ask about our hymns are not are they old or new—that shouldn't really come into it—but do they glorify God? Are they Biblically sound? Can they be sung easily by the congregation or are they just for performers to play?

Members' meetings

If the church is united, members' meetings can be a joy as you all work together with a single aim and purpose. But often they are the place for disgruntled members of the congregation to voice their criticisms in a public way in order to gain support from others. The AOB section is always a bit of a minefield. No wonder it is called 'Any Other Bombs' by pastors!

My experience was mixed. The bad ones were times of great discouragement, not only to me but also to other members of the church. After one meeting, where a few had been voicing their 'righteous indignation' about some of the modern hymns I had introduced, one member called me up the following morning deeply distressed at what he had heard the night before, saying, 'I had no idea we were so disunited.' These 'discussions' can often do more harm than good and create disunity rather than the intended togetherness.

The worst members' meeting occurred when two members were shouting across the room at each other, which was a continuation of an altercation they had had in the church car park a week or two before. It was hard to stop the row once it got going. It was honestly a disgrace in the sight of God for two Christians to be behaving in such an aggressive manner. Thankfully everyone else kept quiet as I tried, with little success, to act as a peacemaker. One lady came up to me afterwards and said, 'I can't take any more. When you leave, I leave.'

I learned to be careful about the AOB section. I asked the congregation to write to me a week before the meeting if they had anything they wanted to discuss. I then said I'd mention it to the rest of the leadership and we would decide if it merited a public discussion or not. This generally worked well. Most of the requests could be dealt with beforehand and so there was no need to spend time on them during the meeting. It also gave me the opportunity to think about any reply I wanted to give and to seek the advice of the other leaders and, most importantly, to pray. Some of the requests were so trivial that I was pleased not to have to deal with them before the whole congregation.

These meetings were useful for me to set out my vision for the church, to detail what had been happening, and to deal with any requests or misunderstandings. Most of the congregation were satisfied with that, but I found there were always a few who were spoiling for a public fight over some minor issue.

Lessons

- It is better to have too much control in members' meetings than too little. As mentioned above, a few difficult people can make life tough if they are allowed to complain publicly about anything from the length of the sermon to women being permitted to hand out the offering bags.

- Try not to take comments personally. If someone does complain about the length of your sermons, it doesn't necessarily mean they hate your preaching. It might just be that your sermons are too long, so consider shortening them. Remember the saying all preachers should take seriously, 'Stand up, speak up, shut up!' And always keep a sense of humour and proportion.

- Take requests from members seriously, but do not feel compelled to bring everything they mention before the church. Deal with time-

Chapter 3

wasting, distracting requests courteously but firmly, otherwise the congregation end up setting the agenda; but never forget that members' meetings are for the members.

- Take great care over the AOB section. It really can create many more problems than it solves. My advice would be to get rid of it altogether.

- Beware of allowing the same individual to speak into every situation, so that one person does not exercise too much influence.

- It is helpful to have a fairly lengthy time of prayer after the meeting, if only to reset everyone's focus back onto the Lord. It also helps to calm down any frayed nerves or agitated spirits.

Charismatic issues

'The slightest whiff of anything Charismatic and I'm off.' That's how I was greeted one day by a member of my church. I think it was in response to a new hymn I had introduced. My church was a million miles away from being Charismatic. I had no intention of making it Charismatic and the congregation were happy with that. However, we did have a small number who were positively anti-Charismatic, so if they detected anything that in their eyes could be leaning in that direction they were ready to raise the roof in protest.

Let me mention a few examples. Shortly after I became the pastor a lovely lady joined the church who had come from a less rigid church background. There is no way she could be described as Charismatic but she did occasionally lift one hand up about halfway during a hymn if she found it inspirational. A less offensive lady you could not care to meet. Yet a member came to me and said, 'Can you please tell "so and so" not to raise her hand in worship as we are not that kind of church.' My response was immediate. 'I can't do that,' I said politely but firmly. 'She is just worshipping the Lord and there's nothing wrong with that.' Someone else thought that anyone who raised their hands in worship was just trying to draw attention to themselves and caused a distraction to everyone else. I said, 'Well, they don't distract me.' By the way, the lady mentioned above was the only person who ever raised a hand.

Fairly early on I got the members who came to the prayer meeting to sit in a circle when we prayed. I felt it was better for everyone to be looking at each other when they shared prayer requests and it made it easier to hear what someone prayed, especially as many in the congregation were elderly. Most people had no problem with this arrangement, except for one couple who found it impossible to sit in the circle because it reminded them of the Charismatic church. So they sat on their own, outside the circle.

Some of the songs that were on my organist's forbidden list (mentioned above) were in her eyes too Charismatic, which is one of the reasons why she refused to play them. A couple of members were aggressive cessationists, even thanking God in prayer that the gifts of the Spirit were no longer operational. I realised almost immediately that their prayers were a horizontal sermon to the other members. I am not a cessationist, but not once did I try to encourage any exercise of any of the 'gifts of the Spirit'. What I didn't like was their attempt to influence other members of the church when they were meant to be praying to God. It was a misuse or abuse of prayer.

Lessons

- It is important to stick to your beliefs and principles although you do not have to impose them on others, especially in controversial and non-essential areas of Christian doctrine. I was happy to 'agree to disagree without being disagreeable' with those who held different opinions. It does become difficult, however, when certain members try to push forward their own theological agenda on the congregation and use underhand methods to achieve their goal.

- If someone does step out of line in this area, the pastor is well within his rights to have a polite private chat with the individual, not necessarily to convince him that what he believes is wrong, but to ask him to refrain from expressing controversial views in the public meetings of the church.

- So many churches have split over the Charismatic issue that it is best left alone as far as possible. I would never advise a Charismatic pastor to enter a Reformed church with the view of changing it. Nor would I advise a Reformed minister to go to a Charismatic church with the express desire of 'reforming' it. Division and chaos will follow and God will not be glorified.

- Try to make a clear distinction in your own mind between what is purely evangelical tradition and what is Biblical. Sometimes these two areas can get blurred. Is it Biblical to raise your hands in worship or is it merely traditional? Is it Biblical for everyone to worship in exactly the same manner or is there room for diversity in the same congregation? Is it traditional to stand for worship or Biblical? And so on.

- I do not believe we can dictate how an individual Christian worships God. It is not up to us to say you must raise your hands or you must keep your hands down. Only if someone is acting like an exhibitionist do we have that right.

Women

Here is another 'hot' topic, but also one that is very relevant to the church today. I only want to talk about my experiences, so I will leave most of the debate alone. The situation I inherited did not leave much room for women to exercise a ministry in the church. They were allowed to be Sunday school teachers, pianists, caterers and flower arrangers, but that was about it.

An interesting event took place which will give you an idea of how the church had been run. I was away one Sunday and one of my deacons, who was a little more 'modern' than some in the church, asked his wife to do the Bible reading in the morning service. This obviously upset my predecessor because I heard he went to another church in the evening because he was worried a woman might read the Scriptures again. This stood out because he never went to another church and would never miss a meeting. I am not going into the wrongs and rights of what happened but it will give you a flavour of the type of opinions and practices I inherited.

Now I am not advocating women in leadership. My opinion is that the Lord raises up men for those roles. But I do not have a problem with a woman reading the Bible in a service or of taking up the offering, for instance. By the time I left I was pleased to have a lady running the data projection equipment in the services and a lady treasurer. Unfortunately, I did not have the nerve to ask a woman to read the Scriptures in a service. I erred on the side of caution. I did not want to stir up unnecessary trouble. Perhaps I was wrong to be so reticent.

What always mystified me was that the men who did not want a woman taking any part in a *Sunday* service, allowed a lady missionary to speak at the *Tuesday* service and did not forbid their wives to pray in the prayer meeting or to speak in a members' meeting, sometimes in an aggressive and unhelpful way. What is the difference? We are in the presence of God, worshipping him, whether it's a Sunday, Tuesday or Thursday, and God's Word does not change according to the day of the week.

Lessons

- We all have our own views about the role of women in the church, but we need to be consistent in our beliefs and to explain them carefully before the church, so the members at least understand the position we hold. Once again I could have been more communicative and less worried about confrontation.

Chapter 3

- Women have vital roles to fill in the church and must be used to their maximum and fully appreciated at all times.

- One has to think carefully before pushing women into controversial areas of service. Is it worth the aggravation that it will stir up for the women themselves and for the church?

- As pastors we must never look down on the role of women or portray a superior attitude towards them. Perhaps we can learn from this amusing anecdote: 'A young man went into a bookshop and asked the girl behind the counter if she had a book called *Man, the master of women*? The girl tossed her head and replied, 'You'll have to look for that in the fiction department!'

- I will allow myself another funny story to help us value the women in our church. A Sunday school teacher asked a girl if she knew the story of Adam and Eve. 'Yes,' replied the girl. 'First God created Adam and then looked at him and said, "I think I can do better." So he created girls!'

- If we disagree with something that goes on in the church, it is not the right approach to skulk off to another church. If we all did that, it would be chaos. There are too many church hoppers as it is.

Visiting missionaries

After I had been at the church for a while I realised that we had been supporting a missionary in a far-off land for some twenty years, but she had never had a visit from anyone in the church. When I asked why no one had visited, I was told that because she attended a more Charismatic type church in her country of service, the previous pastor had felt uncomfortable about going. I was undeterred and thought it was about time we visited her. As she was a single lady missionary I knew my wife had to come with me. I put the case to the leaders and they were supportive. They agreed the church would pay my expenses and I was quite excited about going.

That was before my treasurer (mentioned above) got involved. She was adamant that the church could not afford to send me and seemed to suggest that I was just wanting some sort of 'joy ride'. The church at that time had more than £50,000 just sitting in its account, plus a huge manse fund. I took a pragmatic approach and said I was prepared to pay for my wife out of my own pocket. Some of the church members strongly objected to this suggestion as they did not feel it was my responsibility to pay for 'church work'. In the end, because of the treasurer's objections, I was happy for individuals in the church to make personal donations towards the trip and I would pay the remainder. As it happened we received more than sufficient money to pay for the trip and donated the remainder to our missionary and the cause for which she was working. This meant the treasurer had no cause to complain because we had not used a penny of the church's reserves.

However, the treasurer managed to get the church to vote on whether or not I should be allowed to go. What was particularly upsetting was that she drafted in her two children, who were members but were away at university. Although they had not attended previous members' meetings, they followed their mother's instructions and voted against my proposed visit, along with her husband and one or two close friends. Thankfully the result was overwhelmingly positive and we prepared to go, although the whole process left an unpleasant taste in our mouths.

It was such a profitable time. Not only were we able to see first-hand our missionary's living conditions and the exact nature of her work (cross cultural training, teaching English, translation work, writing, taking Bible studies and orientation courses, etc.) but we were able to chat to the leader of her team and other members to get a fuller picture of what she was doing and how well she was doing it. Nothing was more helpful in our assessment than these impartial opinions. We also struck up a friendship with our missionary that lasts to this day. Our visit proved to

Chapter 3

her how much we loved and supported her as a church and, according to her own admission, we were a great encouragement and blessing to her, giving her new resolve to continue the fight. I also had the immense privilege of preaching in her church before its vast congregation of many thousands.

When we returned home, we gave the church a detailed account of all we had done and seen, and informed the congregation more fully of all that our missionary was doing in the name of the Lord. This in turn enthused them to continue their support, both prayerfully and financially.

Lessons

- Nothing can replace a personal visit to the missionaries the church supports. Letters, skype, emails, zoom, etc., can never give you the 'sights, sounds and smells' of the real life of your missionary as he or she works in a far-off land.

- Any respected member of the church can visit a missionary; it does not have to be the pastor. In my case, there was no one else able or willing to go.

- If you are giving regular sums of money to any individual, it makes perfect sense to ensure that they are doing what the church is expecting them to do. It is an opportunity to assess their work, make suggestions, listen to their complaints and hardships and to get to know them personally, rather than just as a name on the account's sheet. Accountability is important. Our visit gave us the chance to listen to our missionary as she poured out her heart, with tears, over some of the hurts, pains and struggles she was encountering.

- Try to put yourself in the shoes of the missionary. Would you like a visit from your home church? Would it not show you how much they cared and were interested in your service? I'm sure it would be a huge tonic to your morale.

- When you return home, it is a wonderful opportunity to inform and enthuse the church, not only about your particular missionary, but about the work of missions in general and to look for other charities to support.

- Don't be surprised if there are some in the church who do not understand the point and expense of flying thousands of miles to visit a missionary. Maybe they think you are just going on a 'jolly'. It may well be the older members, who have a rather outdated view of missionary work, who say to themselves, 'Missionaries should sail off into the sunset, never to return home and never to be seen again this side of glory.'

Sabbatical

I'm sure there are some people in the church who think a Sabbatical for the pastor is totally unnecessary, especially if they themselves have worked hard in their jobs for many years without any hope of getting extra paid time off. I can understand that. I worked for twenty-five years as a teacher without any Sabbatical. I just accepted it; but the pastorate is different. I had a Sabbatical written into my church contract, either half a Sabbatical after three and a half years, or a full Sabbatical to be taken some time in the seventh year. That's all it said. It did not mention the length of time or the purpose of the Sabbatical, which meant that all the details had to be negotiated nearer the time.

One of the big problems I found in the pastorate was that so much of what you have to do is written with invisible ink on a blank piece of paper. By that I mean, you get up in the morning and you can do precisely what you want to do, especially if you are the only employee. No one is watching over you or telling you what to do. You do as you think best. If you want to stay in bed till 10 o'clock then no one stops you. If you want to work through the night with no sleep, no one is there to say 'it's bedtime'.

Chapter 3

It was pretty much the same with my Sabbatical. I could take it when I wanted, for as long as I wanted and do what I wanted. No one was there to advise or guide me. Now that might sound like the dream scenario, but in all good conscience you want to do what is right before the Lord, for the church and for yourself.

The FIEC have various recommendations when it comes to taking a Sabbatical, but at my church no one was really interested in talking about the different possibilities. So I took half a Sabbatical after about four years. I took a number of weeks off and it was a time to rest and recharge the batteries. Did I really need it? Probably not, in hindsight. Did the church object to my taking one? No. Did it do me any good spiritually? Only in the sense that my times with the Lord were less pressurised. Was it therefore a waste of time? As far as the church was concerned, probably. As far as I was concerned, it was a great time of relaxation.

The one thing I did notice was that after my Sabbatical the church was never quite the same. Now I don't have any concrete reasons for saying that and cannot specifically put my finger on what had changed, but things just seemed different. No one said anything negative to me at the time, so I can only guess. Whether the previous pastor objected, I don't know. What I do know is that he had to be persuaded to take a Sabbatical after about ten years of service. He did not like to leave the church, because he was worried about what might happen to it while he was away. He feared a Charismatic influence might come in if he was not there on sentry duty, so I have been told.

Do I regret taking a Sabbatical so early in my ministry? Yes and no. From a personal point of view I had a restful time. But it might not have been best for the church, something I did not fully realise at the time. Perhaps the church needed a longer time of stability. Perhaps I had to prove my dedication and commitment. Perhaps the congregation missed me and felt a bit despondent without me. These are all guesses. What I do know is that if I had my time again, I would wait until my seventh year before considering a Sabbatical.

There is one aspect of my Sabbatical that I do regret. We had a lovely elderly lady in the church who was gracious and supportive of my ministry, and we struck up a good relationship. Sadly, while I was on my Sabbatical she died. So I asked myself the question, 'Do I return from my Sabbatical to take her funeral?' I spoke to my elder about it and he thought there was no point having a Sabbatical if it was continually interrupted. He also said there was another minister, who had known the family for years, who might be prepared to take the service. So we agreed that if he was happy to take the funeral, I would stay away. If he was not, I would return and conduct it. As it happened he was willing and so I stayed away.

So what do I regret? Although I was out of town at the time, I should have returned and at least attended the service. We were only about an hour and a half away, so the distance was not an obstacle. She was a dear lady and a faithful member and I should have been there to support the family and to show my last respects. Subsequently I found out that one of my members was upset I did not return for the service. I am still sorry to this day that I missed her final goodbye.

Lessons

- My advice would be to have a Sabbatical written into your contract, specifying when it is to be taken, for how long and its precise purpose.

- If you are unsure about taking a Sabbatical and there is no one in the church to consult about the matter, then chat to several other senior pastors and see what they counsel.

- I would err on the side of caution and only take a Sabbatical when it is needed or according to your contract. There may be some in your congregation who do not believe in the principle of a Sabbatical and so resent your having, what in their eyes, is an extra and unnecessary holiday.

Chapter 3

- Think carefully about the best way to use your Sabbatical: perhaps as a time of rest, additional training and study, visiting missionaries, preaching at other churches. The questions to ask are: will my Sabbatical do me good and will it benefit my church?

- While a Sabbatical is important, it is not more important than people. So if there is an emergency in the church, such as a death, then it would be wise to be ready to break into your rest time so you can help in whatever way is required.

- Consider having a study month each year instead of a Sabbatical. Some pastors find this more useful and it is less disruptive to a congregation.

4. So called 'friendly fire'

We all know what 'friendly fire' means—when you are shot at by your own side. Sadly, this is all too common in churches.

Conflict between members

I must admit this is one area I never thought too much about before becoming a pastor. As a teacher I often had to deal with children arguing and falling out. Occasionally I had to deal with teachers having difficulties with each other and once in a while with parents who had 'come to blows'. So I wasn't a complete novice. But conflict between church members was a different kettle of fish. There was no workplace professionalism, no church policy to deal with fights between members, no rule book to consult, no hierarchy and little submission. Now of course you might say, 'Well, what about the Bible? That's our rule book!' I wholeheartedly agree. But it is not always easy to get your members to obey its precepts. For instance, the Bible tells us to forgive from the heart. So why are there resentments in the life of some church members towards those who sit across the aisle?

One of the disadvantages of a small church is that everyone tends to be on top of each other, working in a confined space with the inability to hide differences. It's hard to avoid that individual who has 'ruffled your feathers'. This inevitably means there will be personality clashes and fall-outs between members. What I hadn't realised is how often they can occur and how it affects the whole church as everyone seems to find out about the latest squabble. A great deal of time, stress and energy can be used up trying to resolve problems between two Christians who don't really want to 'kiss and make up'. It can also mean, if things are not handled wisely, that you end up in the middle, with both combatants turning their fire on you instead.

Chapter 4

We had an incident where two men fell out (while I was away) because one of them took some photographs of an event that was taking place in the church. He had not asked or received permission, and although I think he did it innocently and out of enthusiasm for what was going on, the other brother took great exception to him for taking pictures of his son, who was about six years old. A mighty rumpus greeted me when I returned to the church. I spoke to both parties, wrote both a friendly letter, tried to pour water on the flames, but with little success. Although the situation improved, it was never fully resolved and the relationship between those two men was never the same. Later on it erupted again, with one of the men accusing the other of looking inappropriately at his wife. Did they appreciate my involvement? No! One of them thought I had handled it badly and did not think it was necessary for me to 'interfere'. All this bad feeling slightly soured the atmosphere in the church.

Another incident was more theological. One of our members was a zealous Calvinist and he would do all he could to convince all and sundry that his understanding of the Bible was the correct one. May I add at this point that I regard myself as a 'gentle Calvinist'. This particular individual discovered that a relatively new member was not so strong on the 'five points' as he was, so endeavoured to 'convert' him. So much so that every time he came to the church he accosted the new member with books, leaflets, lectures, Bible verses, etc. He even got one of his friends to join ranks to pursue his 'victim'. The new member was having none of it and gave as good as he got, but he became so fed up with them waiting for him at the church door, that he and his wife crept in through a side entrance.

As can be imagined, these confrontations became heated at times. In the end the new member just blanked the zealous Calvinist, which did not go down well. The new member came to me quite upset, and could not understand why such behaviour was allowed to continue. He wanted me to throw this man out of the church. Wisely or unwisely I decided to 'bury my head in the sand' and hoped the situation would resolve itself. I did not think I could kick the Calvinist out of the church, and knowing him

So-called 'friendly fire'

as I did, the more I told him to be quiet, the more he would try to convert others. Did it ever get resolved? It certainly quieted down, but another relationship was fractured.

On one occasion a couple in the church held a combined 80th birthday celebration. We arranged an afternoon tea in the church hall and encouraged members to invite their friends and neighbours, a few of whom came. Everything was running smoothly until down the far end of the hall a loud commotion erupted. I quietly slipped away from my guests holding my breath. In the church itself two non-members were having a right set to and hurling abuse at each other. Apparently a couple with two young children had sat down next to a lady who, unbeknown to them, hated children. During the meal one of the youngsters threw some food across the table which accidentally hit this lady. She lost her rag and accused the parents of failing to control their 'brats'. It then sparked off into a full blown row. By the time I arrived they were nearly coming to blows. As can be imagined I felt so embarrassed for the non-Christians who had attended the 'happy celebration'.

As I write this I can't help chuckling to myself as I remember how a little spark can set the whole church blazing. James was right when he said, 'Consider what a great forest is set on fire by a small spark. The tongue also is a fire, a world of evil among the parts of the body. It corrupts the whole person, sets the whole course of his life on fire, and is itself set on fire by hell' (James 3:5–6). Actually, it wasn't funny at all at the time. It was a disgraceful witness to our non-Christian guests and I couldn't help thinking, 'Who would want to join this church?' The lady who hated children soon moved to a different part of the country and the father of the children fell away from the Lord. His wife was not a Christian.

One Tuesday a missionary couple came to speak at the church about their work in an African country. Just after they had finished speaking, and as we were about to pray, one of the members of the congregation started to shout at them, accusing them of hypocrisy. I quickly intervened. Apparently the reason for the man's anger was because this couple, when

Chapter 4

members of another local church, had been instrumental in refusing him funding when he had applied for a church grant to attend Bible College. Although this had happened some ten years before, he was still resentful and felt he had been unfairly treated by them. Actually, the missionary couple were one hundred percent right as there was no one I could think of less suitable for a Bible College education.

My final example regarded a visiting preacher. I had asked a member of the church if he wouldn't mind finding supply preachers for when I was away. I just asked him to check with me first before he invited anyone new. Unfortunately he did not do this and invited a man I did not know, to whom another member took great exception. I spoke to both men and I was happy that the supply preacher was not a 'heretic'. He came, preached a sound sermon and did not upset anyone with his views. Sadly, before the Sunday arrived, the two men, who had taken up theological arms against each other, had a blazing and very public row outside the church, in front of passers-by.

Now you might be thinking that my church was complete chaos all the time. I must say that these incidents were over a period of many years. Thankfully we had long spells of peace.

Lessons

- Don't be surprised or shocked when conflict between members erupts. The church is full of sinners, so it's bound to happen sooner or later. It even happened to Jesus' disciples. Christians still have a sinful nature with which to grapple. The real skill is dealing with it appropriately, pouring water on the flames and bringing about a reconciliation. This of course requires great skill and is easier said than done.

- Think very carefully before stepping in to become a mediator and always take another member of the leadership team with you when making a 'reconciliation' visit. Sometimes your involvement is not necessary. Sometime it causes more trouble than it's worth. Sometimes the

So-called 'friendly fire'

combatants turn their guns on you instead and resent your interference. As someone has said, 'A boy becomes a man when he walks around a puddle instead of through it.'

- Before you jump in to stop a fight, consider the advice of Solomon in Proverbs 26:17: 'Like one who seizes a dog by the ears is a passer-by who meddles in a quarrel not his own.' Leave room for God to deal with his children in his own way and time.

- If you do decide to intervene, take great care to be impartial. It will not help the situation if you take sides and accidentally end up supporting the wrongdoer. And remember the English proverb: 'It takes two to make a quarrel.'

- In your attempts to be impartial remember the saying, 'A long dispute means that both parties are wrong.'

- It might be worth sharing this story with the arguing members: 'In an old monastery near Bebenhausen, Germany, there are a pair of deer horns interlocked. The deer had been fighting, their horns had become jammed together and could not be separated. Both deer died locked together. Dr Kerr, who first told the story, added, "I would like to carry those horns into every church."'

- Try to reason with the combatants that our fight is 'not against flesh and blood' but against the devil (Ephesians 6:12). How can any home or army overcome the enemy if they are fighting among themselves? It's sheer madness and means that we have lost sight of the real foe, who is standing by laughing at the church for being so foolish.

- After any conversation, encourage the members to pray out loud there and then about the situation and about what they are going to do to

The Pastorate

Chapter 4

resolve it. Sometimes focusing their attention onto the Lord helps them to come to their senses.

- In my experience, any relationship that has been damaged by conflict is very hard to put back together, unless there is a real desire for that to happen from both parties.

- I think there comes a time, if two members are quarrelling and upsetting the church and refusing to settle their differences, that one or both must be asked to leave, at least for a time so they can calm down and forgive.

Spitters and head shakers

Now from the title you might be asking the question: what on earth is he going to be talking about now? Let's deal with spitters first. In my church we had two or three members who would accidentally spit when talking to you. So if you got too close, you would get a spray of saliva all over your face. One of the problems was that those who had this unfortunate habit always liked to speak to you at very close quarters. They got in your space, as we say. After I had been drenched a couple of times, I decided to step back surreptitiously to get further away from them whenever they came too close in conversation. They in turn would take a step forward. So I would take another small step back, hoping they wouldn't notice, and they would take another step forward, so we would end up dancing around the church in this manner. The end of the conversation would take place some distance away from where it had started!

Occasionally after I got a face full I would make an 'uhhrr!' noise and wipe my face to try to send out a hint as to what was happening, but they never seemed to catch on. It made me very reluctant to chat with them after church, especially if they had just eaten a biscuit! If I did speak with them, I would encourage them to sit down and I would place my chair a safe distance away from them. Now this is something they do not teach you at Bible College!

So-called 'friendly fire'

If I went to visit them at their own homes, I would make sure I sat further enough away from them to be out of range. Once or twice I naughtily put my wife in the firing line while I sat behind her! (This is the first time I have admitted to this, so I might be in trouble when she reads my account!)

I now come to the head shakers. I will say first of all that every time head shaking is mentioned in the Bible it is in a negative way. For instance, in Psalm 22, that great crucifixion psalm, we read in verse 7: 'All who see me mock me; they hurl insults, shaking their heads.' The fulfilment of that comes in places like Matthew 27:39–40, where those who passed by the cross hurled insults at Christ, shaking their heads and challenging him to come down from the cross if he was the Son of God. In Psalm 64 it says 'all who see them [evildoers] will shake their heads in scorn' (64:8) and Jeremiah 18:16 says, Israel's 'land will be laid waste, an object of lasting scorn; all who pass by will be appalled and will shake their heads'.

My interpretation of people who shake their heads at you is that they disagree with you or, worse, are holding you in contempt. I had one young man in my congregation who was a notorious head shaker. He never came up to me to say anything directly, but in sermons and members' meetings he would shake his head and scowl in such a way that anyone sitting within the confines of the church could see him. After a while this greatly annoyed me as it was a public way of saying, 'Pastor, what you have just said is wrong and I am letting everyone in this church know that I disagree with you.' This kind of behaviour does not give you an opportunity to respond to them, because you can't stop your sermon to find out what his problem might be, although you can politely ask him later.

Lessons

- I really don't have any great insights to pass on regarding spitters except to try to keep well clear of them, unless of course you don't mind having a shower when you are fully clothed! Once in this regard I did

Chapter 4

ask a lady, as politely as I could, to be careful when she spoke to me. Thankfully she did not take offence.

- More seriously though, be gracious in your response. They are not spitting on purpose. Move away slowly so it's not too obvious what you are doing, and if the conversation is likely to be a long one, get them to sit down some distance away from you. I found it much easier when I went to visit these members as I made sure I sat down outside their firing range. I also avoided sitting next to them at meal times.

- As far as head shakers are concerned, I admit I overreacted by getting annoyed, although I never showed it. My advice is to just ignore them and don't let it distract you from what you want to say. Don't let them upset you, because that is what they are probably trying to do. Maybe you could gently go up to them and say something like, 'I noticed you were disagreeing with me during my sermon, would you like to chat about it?' and see what happens next. They may say, 'Oh no, there was no problem' and chicken out of any conversation. But it might stop them from doing the same thing next time.

- Be gracious in your responses to members who annoy you. Maybe the Lord is testing you to see what is in your heart. 'A fool shows his annoyance at once, but a prudent man overlooks an insult' (Proverbs 12:16).

Christmas trees

Now this might seem a strange heading, but we had several in the church who were strongly and vocally opposed to having a Christmas tree in the church. For my first Christmas, about four months after I had started at the church, I did not realise the strength of feeling, and without thinking put up a Christmas tree. By the time Christmas was over their new pastor was labelled a 'pagan and idolater'. These individuals were against Christmas altogether and would not even wish anyone a happy Christmas or send

Christmas cards. They regarded Christmas as a pagan festival and the Christmas tree as a symbol of idolatry.

I didn't really mind them having their opinion, but what made things difficult was the force with which they condemned everyone else who held a different view. They almost regarded those of us who enjoyed Christmas as infidels. One lady argued that her father had always said it was wrong to have a Christmas tree at home or in the church, and he was a Christadelphian!

The majority of people in the church loved Christmas. One lady even told me that she had been converted one Christmas because she had gone into a church and seen a Christmas tree. She suddenly realised that Christians were normal people and that drew her to Christ. Another lady asked if we could put a manger in the church for the carol service. I had no problem with that until a baby doll appeared in it. One man refused to attend the church because of the doll. I went to see him and apologised to him because I thought the empty manger was fine, but I was not happy with the doll and appreciated his opinion on that matter. However, I made the point that it was not the right way to deal with a difference of opinion by refusing to attend the church. One year one of my deacons put a large tree in the church with flashing lights which I admit were a bit of a distraction. I had to turn them off halfway through the service.

How did I deal with all the different opinions regarding Christmas? Well I never managed to convince the vocal minority that the Christmas tree was just a harmless decoration and was not intended to be worshipped. We ended up putting a small tree in the foyer of the church, so it would not be too noticeable, a decision that seemed to appease most people.

Lessons

- What is difficult to deal with is people's overreaction to things they don't like. My advice would be to try and reason with them and to encourage them to be more gracious in their attitude, especially over

Chapter 4

issues where there are lots of different opinions and where they are in the minority.

- Who should dictate what goes on in a church—the pastor, the majority, the vocal minority? The pastor must lead, taking with him as many members as possible. For those who refuse to follow, a gentle word in the ear is more productive than a strong rebuke.

- I think the whole area of submission comes into this argument (Hebrews 13:17).

- Wisdom would suggest trying to find a middle way that will not offend. However, if this proves impossible, a decision will have to be made and the consequences dealt with in a Christ-like manner.

- George Whitefield used to say that he did not argue where there was no hope of persuasion. I think that is a good principle to stand on. What is the point of spending hours debating with someone who will just become more entrenched in their own views? It's just a waste of valuable time.

- Truth without love can be hurtful and hard. Some Christians who hold strong views about non-essential issues act too aggressively. They are too forthright in expressing what they believe to be right and will not give up until they have tried to convince the whole congregation. What we read about Jesus is that he is full of grace and truth. 'For the law was given through Moses; grace and truth came through Jesus Christ' (John 1:17). That's the way to approach all of these controversial areas: with grace and truth.

- It must never be forgotten that there will always be more than one view in the church. As far as Christmas was concerned we had the silent majority. 85% of the members had no problems with celebrating Christmas or with Christmas trees in the church. Unfortunately we only heard the noisy minority.

- Be ready for a few surprises along the way. That first Christmas I was invited round to the house of a couple who I suspected of being anti-Christmas. I could not have been more wrong. When I arrived at their house I could hardly believe it. Every room was full of Christmas decorations and lights. They gave me a lengthy tour, as we examined each corner with all its delights and they enthusiastically told me how they added to their decorations every year.

Criticism and false accusations

I must start by saying that criticism and false accusations are bound to come. We are dealing with sinful pastors, sinful people and a cunning and spiteful enemy in the devil. That combination means that things will be said that are wrong and hurtful, so be prepared.

Let's talk firstly about letters and emails. During my first couple of months of the pastorate I received two letters from an elderly member of the church. The first accused me of treating the congregation like children and the second was a gentle threat of trouble if we dared to sing anything other than the old hymns. As far as the first letter was concerned I thought to myself, 'Well, I've been teaching children for the last twenty-five years, so if what she says is true then it's hardly surprising!' That's what I thought, but I wrote back a friendly letter saying that it had not been my intention to treat adults like children. I also asked the other leaders if I had come across in that way, and they assured me I hadn't.

As I was new to the pastorate, still strong and enthusiastic, these letters did not affect me, but I did speak with my predecessor. I told him about the letters and asked whether it was normal to receive them. He just raised his eyes to the heavens and exclaimed, 'Oh, the letters!' That was all he said. I took that to mean that he had received quite a few during his

Chapter 4

time and they were not easy to deal with. Perhaps I should have taken his response as a warning that there would be more flying my way.

It is just human nature that we rarely get letters of encouragement thanking us for this or that, but we get plenty of moaning letters. People can be quite bold in a letter or email, saying things they would never say to your face. It's keyboard bravery from keyboard warriors!

Perhaps the most vicious letter I received was in a resignation letter. I can't remember all that the woman said, but she accused me of various things as well as saying that I showed no signs of the fruit of the Spirit. She was basically saying I wasn't even a Christian. I must admit I struggled for a time to recover from that one. She gave a copy to all the leaders. My two deacons were shocked by its contents and wrote letters to the woman, expressing their dismay at its contents. My elder just ignored it. One of the deacons showed it to a member who had come round for lunch and this lady exclaimed after she read it, 'Where is the love?'

The problem with this particular letter was that it came when I was low in spirits anyway. It is just like the devil to kick us when we are down. I was given the letter after the morning service. It floored me. It was the only time in my pastorate that I felt I could not climb the two steps up to the pulpit and preach a sermon that evening. I called up one of my deacons and told him how I felt and asked if he could preach for me at short notice. He said he did not have a sermon available, so I was left to give it a go. Amazingly, the verses I had prepared to preach on were Psalm 118:13–14: 'I was pushed back and about to fall, but the Lord helped me. The Lord is my strength and my song; he has become my salvation.' I certainly felt as though I was 'about to fall' but the Lord 'helped me'.

I have never found it so hard to preach as that evening. Everything within me cried out to be somewhere else. I could hardly open my mouth. It was as if I was somewhere else, dreaming about preaching. I had no idea what I was really saying, but it obviously made sense. One of my deacons, who had read the letter and knew my state of mind, was quite moved by the sermon and commented (a bit tongue in cheek), 'That sermon was so good I wish you were always hurting.' The lady member who had seen the letter said that she had great admiration for me after I had preached in such pain.

But criticism can also come through the spoken word. Again, rarely do people come up to you to criticise something you've said or done. It is more normal for them to tell someone else. You, of course, eventually get to hear most of what has been said and the accusations that have been laid at your door. Some are really quite damaging if they are believed by others. Some are hurtful. The trouble is, even if they are completely untrue the mud has a tendency to stick. In my time as pastor I was falsely accused of all sorts of things, but only by two or three people.

On an aside, one noticeable difference between the criticism I received at school and the criticism I received at church was that the church criticism was always much more personal. At school, if something went wrong in the classroom or between children, it was usually the 'school's' fault. The criticism was more general and it was as if the parents tried hard not to make things too personal. At church it was the opposite. As soon as something went wrong, it was 'my' fault. I was responsible. It seemed that Christians were much more likely to attack you as a person rather than something you might have done. This of course raises the stakes and makes the criticism more difficult to handle. If you're not careful, you can begin to doubt your own personality! That's my observation and experience anyway.

But false accusations can do immense harm. I remember hearing about a young couple who were happily married. Then the village gossip got to work. She started to whisper rumours that the husband was playing around with other women, which was completely untrue. At first no one believed her, but as she persisted, dropping a hint here and there, opinions of the husband began to change. The wife then heard about the rumours and felt a little uneasy about what might be going on behind her back. She became suspicious. When the husband found out about what people were saying about him, he was so shocked and dismayed

Chapter 4

that he hanged himself. A marriage was ruined and a life destroyed by false accusations.

This might be the most appropriate time to share about one of my deacons. He was a lovely gracious man, who was popular in the church. He had been a pastor quite a few years before and he was eldership material. After a few years I approached him about becoming an elder and he was keen on the idea. We prayed and I got the leaders and church to pray as well. The one area that I felt uneasy about was the way he greeted people at church. He was a lovable character and he liked to give people a hug, including the ladies, as they entered church. He had received one or two complaints about this behaviour. The problem was not really the hugging, but the length of the hugs. They were a bit too passionate, too long, making one or two feel uncomfortable. I warned him to be very careful as sometimes what we do innocently can be misinterpreted. I think he did try to rein in his 'cuddly' character.

About one week before the church voted on his eldership, this deacon went to the church in the middle of the week to collect some materials. One of the lady members happened to be there at the time cleaning the church. The deacon, in his usual way, greeted her loudly and gave her a big hug. Unfortunately his greeting was not well received and she accused him of sexual harassment, which of course is a criminal offence. When this got back to me I was horrified. I knew I just couldn't leave it alone, so I took another leader with me and went to have a chat with the deacon. He was shocked by the accusation, but the long and short of it was he never returned to the church. I had lost a future elder. I must say after a careful investigation I believe this man to have been entirely innocent in his actions, but unwise. He should have listened to my warnings and not left himself open to unwarranted accusations.

There was one old lady in the church who every time she came to speak to me it was to voice some criticism. It happened so often that when I saw her approaching, I thought to myself, 'Uh-oh, here we go!' and I was never disappointed. This went on for years until I finally cracked and told her about her critical attitude. The next time she approached me I was pleasantly surprised when she complimented something I had done in the church. But before I had a chance to breathe a sigh of relief, she returned to type and immediately followed up her compliment with various criticisms. I don't think she could actually help it. It was her mind-set and had become the norm for her. However, it is not a pleasant attitude for a Christian to have and is not helpful in a church. D. L. Moody said, 'Don't go to church just to criticise. Anyone can do that. If you feel inclined to criticise, just stop and ask yourself whether you could do it any better. Some make only one mistake: that of finding imperfections in everybody and everything' (*D. L. Moody—A Life*, Kevin Belmonte, p. 216).

Sometimes (perhaps I should say usually) criticisms and complaints are unjustified. I remember one young man in my church who could not agree with the church's constitution. When I asked him why, he said it was because of the suggestion by the FIEC that a church should vote on whether or not to close if the membership falls below seven. He was adamantly opposed to a church closing for any reason. He went on to tell me of a church he knew whose membership had fallen to just two old ladies, with no pastor. Apparently these two old ladies kept the church alive by meeting together for prayer for a number of years before others joined them and a new pastor was eventually appointed. I couldn't help thinking that in my view two women meeting together for prayer does not constitute a church. The church had already closed.

Lessons

- It's best not to reply to a critical letter or email but to have a face to face chat with the writer. This is a much friendlier way and may solve the problem in one go, rather than sending emails back and forth that might be misunderstood and become increasingly tense. As someone has said, emails can't smile.

Chapter 4

- It might be worth mentioning to your congregation that 'any jackass can kick down a barn, but it takes a good carpenter to build one'.

- Think carefully and with humility about any personal criticism you receive. As Gordon MacDonald said, 'I have seldom ever heard a criticism about myself that didn't indeed contain a kernel of useful truth.'

- As I've said before, never forget that our struggle is not against flesh and blood. We must direct own energies in fighting our real enemy rather than members of our congregation.

- In any conflict situation our fellowship with the Lord is absolutely vital. Whatever happens, always make it a reason to draw near to the Lord, never to run away from him. There are so many Scriptures in the Bible that help us to understand the value of suffering. Look them up, meditate on them, hold them close to your heart.

- It's important to dispel any rumours as quickly as possible before they take root. Do all that you can to prove your innocence, not so much to protect your reputation, but for the protection of the church and the glory of God. God blesses the truth. 'If men speak ill of you, live so that no one will believe them.'

- Try not to respond in kind. If someone has hurt you through lying gossip, it might be hard to take it quietly, but responding in kind will not achieve harmony. Remember, 'hurt people hurt people'. As someone has said, 'To reply to a nasty remark with another nasty remark is like trying to remove dirt with mud.' I tended to go into my shell rather than come out fighting. I think it would have been better, with another trusted leader, to meet the accusations head on and to discuss them with the accuser. Remember a 'gossip separates close friends' (Proverbs 16:28) and 'without gossip a quarrel dies down' (Proverbs 26:20).

- As it says in Proverbs, 'Above all else, guard your heart, for it is the wellspring of life' (4:23). Don't let anger or bitterness take root (Hebrews 12:15). This is often what your opponent wants and it only damages your walk with the Lord and your ministry to the people.

- 'Avoid every appearance of evil' and any behaviour that is questionable or that can be misinterpreted. Never put yourself in a compromising position and always treat the ladies in your church with the utmost respect and propriety (1 Timothy 5:2). And remember, not everyone likes to be hugged. If my deacon had listened to my advice, he would have become my elder. Having said that, the Lord sometimes moves in a mysterious way to accomplish his purposes.

Words

I write this as a separate heading because words are so important. They can do so much good and so much evil. In my pastorate words have wonderfully encouraged me, saved souls, lifted up the downcast, rebuked sinners, instructed the ignorant and many other praiseworthy things. 'Kind words' are indeed 'the music of the world'. But words have also depressed me, angered me and were probably one of the reasons I left the pastorate. As someone has said, 'The tongue is but three inches long yet it can kill a man six feet tall.'

Let me illustrate how powerful words are by speaking about a small word of just three letters. You have probably heard of the 'wicked' Bible (sometimes called the sinner's Bible or the adulterer's Bible). It was published in 1631 by the royal printers as a reprint of the King James Version. But a big mistake was made. The seventh commandment read: 'Thou shalt commit adultery'—the little word 'not' had been accidentally omitted. As you can imagine it caused outrage. Charles I was horrified.

Chapter 4

The publishers were fined £50,000 (by today's standards) and deprived of their printing licence. It was just one little word, but what an effect it had! The Bible, the most loved and hated book in the world, is made up of words. Our salvation, almost certainly, came about because of words (from a preacher, a friend, or from the words written in the Bible).

In my pastorate I sometimes caused trouble by the words I spoke, either because they were misunderstood or because I spoke unadvisedly or responded to criticism in an ungodly fashion. On a number of occasions the preaching of the gospel caused offence. Spoken or written words are extremely powerful and can do lasting good or cause a great deal of harm.

Lessons

- Never underestimate the power of words. They can have such an effect for good or evil. If you want to know how powerful words are, then listen to these words and notice their effect: 'And God *said*, "Let there be light," and there was light.' 'Jesus *called* in a loud voice, "Lazarus, come out!" The dead man came out.'

- Three verses from the Bible are worth quoting and remembering: Proverbs 25:11 says, 'A word aptly spoken is like apples of gold in settings of silver'—beautiful and valuable. The second and third verses really make you think: 'But I tell you [says Jesus] that men will have to give account on the day of judgment for every careless word they have spoken. For by your words you will be acquitted, and by your words you will be condemned' (Matthew 12:36–37).

- Read James 3 to remind yourself of the power of the tongue.

- 'Sticks and stones may break my bones but words will never hurt me'—rubbish! Words can destroy.

So-called 'friendly fire'

- Take great care how you speak to the members of your congregation. One wrong word, or a word said in the wrong tone, can stir up so much aggravation against your person and ministry. Always try to bite your tongue if you sense a rash word is about to escape. And remember, 'When you have nothing to say, say nothing' (C. Colton).

- The devil is a master at exaggeration and twisting the meaning of the words we speak. Donald Grey Barnhouse rightly said, 'It is a sad fact that the tongues of professing Christians are often all too busy doing the devil's work.'

- Spurgeon, in his inimitable way, said, 'Some men's tongues bite more than their teeth.'

- Words that have been spoken can never be recalled. A sixteenth-century preacher, faced with a woman who confessed to being a slanderer, asked her, 'Do you frequently fall into this fault?' 'Yes, very often,' replied the woman. 'Your fault is great but God's mercy is greater,' said the preacher. 'Go to the nearest market and purchase a freshly killed chicken still covered with its feathers. You will then walk a certain distance, plucking the bird as you go along. When you finish your work return to me here.' The woman did as the preacher instructed and returned, anxious for an explanation. 'Ah,' said the preacher, 'you've been faithful to the first part of my instructions. Now retrace your steps and gather up all the feathers you have scattered.' 'But I can't,' protested the woman. 'I cast them carelessly on every side and the wind carried them in every direction. How can I recover them?' 'And so it is with your words of slander,' said the preacher. 'Like the feathers, they have been scattered and cannot be recalled. Go and sin no more.' (Alistair Begg, *Pathway to Freedom*, pp. 181–182).

5. Battles within

Sometimes the battles that rage within our hearts and minds are much more difficult to deal with than the 'enemy' who stands in front of us cursing and accusing us.

Temptation

I believe one of the reasons why pastors are vulnerable to temptations is because they spend a lot of time of their own, thinking, praying, studying. We are always vulnerable when we are on our own. This is probably one of the reasons why Jesus sent out his disciples in twos. If you think of a gazelle in the African savannah who gets separated from the rest of the herd, that gazelle is in real danger from 'roaring lions'.

I think my areas of greatest temptation were anger at some of the things that people said and did, and despair because the work did not always go in the way I had planned or desired. I tended to mull things over too much. There was too much after-reflection about the things I'd done or how my sermons were received or what people might or might not be thinking. As I have said previously, I think I am too sensitive to be an ideal pastor, without the skin of a rhinoceros!

Lessons

- Fellowship with other Christians is vital. Try to be on your own for as little time as possible. During my pastorate another pastor, who was aware of the temptations that creep up on us when we are alone, came to me and suggested that we should hire a room somewhere so that several pastors could use it as an office. In that way we could work 'together' and not be so isolated. Unfortunately that excellent idea never materialised.

- Take practical steps to avoid temptation. Legend has it that Sirens were sea nymphs who could charm a listening sailor with song. The listener was seized with an irresistible desire to throw himself into the sea to his destruction. Ulysses, once passing their coast, ordered the ears of his seamen to be sealed with wax, while he himself was tied to a post. No matter how much he pleaded or threatened, no one was to release him. As they approached the enchanting coast, ravishing music was heard so that Ulysses struggled and begged to be free, but his sailors bound him more tightly. When they had passed, Ulysses' sanity returned. He was released and his sailors' ears unsealed. Sometimes we need to put wax in our ears and to tie ourselves down so as to resist temptation effectively.

- This quote from Richard Sibbes has been a great help to me: 'Satan gives Adam an apple and takes away Paradise. Therefore in all temptations let us consider not what he offers, but what we shall lose.' When we give in to temptations we never win.

- Share your temptations with others. In *James* we read: 'Confess your sins to each other and pray for each other so that you may be healed. The prayer of a righteous man is powerful and effective' (James 5:16). If we are to confess our sins to each other, we must also confess our temptations.

- The trouble with temptation is that it can keep knocking on your door and you have to keep resisting it again and again. During the pandemic I caught COVID. One of the side effects was a persistent cough. This in turn led to a collection of mucus forming in the back of my throat, which I could not shift and which made it hard to swallow. I did not know what to do until I read the NHS advice sheet on throat clearing. Apparently constant throat clearing produces mucus which makes you want to cough, which then produces more mucus and so the cycle goes

Chapter 5

on. The answer is to break the habit of throat clearing. But that is not an easy habit to break. I felt like clearing my throat all the time. So I followed the advice and gargled with salt water, drank little sips of water, sucked a sugar free sweet, yawned and so on until the mucus stopped forming and the urge to clear my throat lessened. I can tell you it was not easy to resist the urge to clear my throat. But it reminded me of temptation that keeps pulling us towards sin. It is not always easy to resist. We need the grace and power of God, and to take sensible practical steps to avoid it.

- Make no provision for the flesh. Do *not* be like the little boy who was sternly told by his mum never to swim in the lake he passed when walking to school. One night he had a friend over to stay and in the morning the friend saw him packing his swimming trunks into his school bag. 'Why are you packing your swimming trunks?' asked the friend. 'There is no swimming at school today.' 'Oh,' replied the little boy, 'it's in case I get tempted on the way to school!' Now that is what we must *not* do!

- Always take your temptations to the Lord. Here are three R's:
  Remember that Jesus has been tempted in every way, just as we are. He is therefore able to understand, sympathise and help (Hebrews 2:18; 4:15–16).
  Run to Jesus for strength against what is attacking you. And if you fall, run to the cross, where the blood of Christ can wash the vilest sin away.
  Resist the devil and he will flee from you (James 4:7).

- When faced with temptation John Owen tells us to 'think of the guilt of sin, that you may be humbled. Think of the power of sin, that you may seek strength against it. Think not of the matter of sin … lest you be more and more entangled'.

Boredom

This might be a surprising topic to discuss because in my time as a pastor practically every other pastor I spoke to said they were rushed off their feet with a hundred and one jobs and tasks to do, with hardly any time to think, let alone get bored. Well, all I can say to that is I must be an oddity, an exception to the rule.

Now I am the first to admit that I get bored easily. I am also not particularly good at thinking up new things to do. I'm not an ideas man. I'm good at keeping up the status quo, but I'm not a pioneer who is always ready to push the boundaries and advance into new undiscovered territory. So when I was just 'left to get on with it' by the church, I struggled after a while to know exactly how I was to move the church forward.

My day was usually spent preparing sermons in the morning. I guarded this time jealously, especially as I had at least three sermons a week to prepare. The afternoons were spent visiting members of my congregation, or meeting up with various people, such as my elder or other pastors. After a while it became monotonous and I needed someone to encourage me to branch out into new areas of service. The mornings became a sermon treadmill and the afternoons were mainly visiting old ladies in their homes. Both of these were necessary, but not particularly exciting or invigorating. This is in no way a criticism of old ladies, more a criticism of my lack of enthusiasm for listening to their stories about their physical ailments.

I found it hard when there was little interaction with my church leaders, who were all older men, faithfully standing at their post but waiting for the discharge trumpet to sound.

Lessons

- A fairly recent survey found that the average adult spends about one-third of his waking life bored!

Chapter 5

- Boredom can be a debilitating and even a dangerous feeling. I read the account of Diana Humphries of Houston, Texas, who ambushed and killed her fourteen year old brother with a .22 rifle. She had also planned to kill her mother and father and herself. When asked why, she sobbed, 'To escape my boredom, because nothing exciting ever happens around here!' She had wanted to end the 'always-tired' routine of her family life.

- While the above example is somewhat extreme, it does highlight the truth in the sayings: 'An idle mind is the devil's playground' and 'the devil makes work for idle hands to do.' *The Living Bible* translates Proverbs 16:27 as 'Idle hands are the devil's workshop; idle lips are his mouthpiece.'

- It would have been helpful if I had had a younger, enthusiastic man with whom to work. But there was no one like that in the church. In a small church such men are hard to come by. If you have any young men in your congregation, they are usually family men who have taxing jobs that take up most of their time and energy.

- If you pastor a small church, and especially if you are the only paid worker, you have to be ready to work on your own most of the time, with little advice or interaction from the congregation.

- Having said that, stimulating company is a must if you are going to keep firing on all cylinders. Usually this company has to be found outside of the church.

- Personally I think it is essential for your wife to be heavily involved in the church, not only as a help-mate and friend, but also as an accountability partner.

Anger and unforgiveness

After what I have said above it seems fitting to deal with this topic next. One of my many weaknesses is that I find it hard to forgive people. I tend to go over and over what they have done or said, and sometimes I magnify their words and actions out of all proportion, which is certainly not helpful in the pastorate. I know this is a weakness and I have pleaded with the Lord to help me forgive those who have wronged me. To a large degree he has helped me, but it has not been easy, nor has there been a 'quick fix'.

When I was a pastor I tried hard to exercise my will to forgive others, but I struggled. In fact, I used to find it annoying when people told me 'forgiveness is an act of the will' because I had tried to 'will' forgiveness but I just couldn't do it. I quoted Scriptures at myself about the importance and necessity of forgiveness, and even threatened myself with verses like Matthew 6:15: 'If you do not forgive men their sins, your Father will not forgive your sins.' I cried out to the Lord to change my heart, and I even asked others how they managed to forgive wrongdoers. But the same offences kept coming back into my mind and I found it difficult not to dwell on them and get angry at the same time. I am ashamed to admit it, but at times I felt hatred towards certain people. I wanted to punish them and would dream up ways of getting revenge. It is not easy to be a loving pastor when these emotions are filling your heart. Sometimes I would justify myself saying, 'Well, I'm sure they have been forgiven by the Lord, so someone has to punish them!' Thankfully I never actually said what I wanted to say to them. God in his grace kept me from that evil.

A real breakthrough came about two years after I had resigned from the pastorate. I was listening to a sermon at church, most of which didn't speak to me in any way. Then towards the end the preacher mentioned something about forgiveness. I can't remember his exact words, but what I came away with was, 'The reason I forgive others is because I love the Lord.' Not because they deserve to be forgiven. Not because

Chapter 5

they have repented, because often they never did, but because I love the Lord. It was as if a light had been turned on and much of the bitterness melted away.

It all sounds so simple. It is, yet it took me a long time to discover it. I'm not saying I will never have a problem again, but I can always turn to this truth and find help and strength in my weakness.

Lessons

- If you are angry, you are not alone. A. D. Hart says, 'Pastors are among the angriest people I work with.' I think one of the reasons why this can be true is because pastors receive a lot of verbal abuse. Be aware and be ready to respond in a God-honouring fashion. Remind yourself of such verses as Matthew 5:11–12: 'Blessed are you when people insult you, persecute you and falsely say all kinds of evil against you because of me. Rejoice and be glad, because great is your reward in heaven, for in the same way they persecuted the prophets who were before you.'

- One missionary wisely said, after spending years under house arrest, 'Bitterness is the wasted emotion.'

- Here is a helpful paragraph from Peter Brain in his book *Going the Distance*: 'Unresolved anger is like a time bomb, which can cripple our initiative, sour our relationships, make our preaching negative, cause us to blame and scapegoat others, and render us unable to receive encouragement from God or other people. One of the big problems with anger is that we can sometimes enjoy being angry with others. Perhaps it's because we feel powerful, or that we can get our own back, or that the expression of our anger makes us feel good. If we enjoy this anger, it leaves us in danger not only of leaving a trail of destruction amongst others and of increasing our own guilt within, but most sadly, of not dealing with the reason for our anger' (p. 84).

- The trouble with anger is that we may do and say things we will later regret. As the saying goes, 'People who fly into a rage always make a bad landing.'

- There is an amusing story about the Italian conductor Toscanini who was known for his ferocious temper. During one rehearsal a flat note caused the genius to grab his valuable watch and smash it beyond repair. Shortly afterwards, he received from his devoted musicians a luxurious velvet lined box containing two watches, one a beautiful gold timepiece, the other a cheap throwaway on which was inscribed, 'For rehearsals only.'

- Remember you can't save face if you lose your head!

- I heard someone say once regarding anger, 'Don't express it because that hurts others. Don't repress it because that hurts yourself. But confess it so God can forgive you.'

- One lesson I learned was that it is very hard to love others with a Christ-like love if you are holding grudges against them.

- There is a big difference between forgiveness and forgetfulness. It is possible to forgive but not forget. At times I got confused and thought I had not forgiven because I had not forgotten.

- In the end God answered my prayers about forgiveness. So do not give up. Keep pleading with the Lord to help you. He will not fail you.

- After I had left the pastorate and joined a new church, a woman who had caused me a great deal of trouble and hurt in my old church suddenly turned up one Sunday morning. At first the old feelings of resentment rose within me, but then I resolved that if she came again the following

Chapter 5

week I would welcome her and shake her by the hand as if nothing had happened. Well, she came and I shook her by the hand with as much grace as I could muster. The thought did flash through my mind that I had just shaken hands with the devil, but I quickly repented! This incident reminded me of Corrie Ten Boom, who managed to shake the hand of a former SS guard who had been so cruel to her when she was in Ravensbrück concentration camp (see Corrie Ten Boom, *The Hiding Place*, pp. 220–221).

- Keep listening to sermons, even the boring ones, because God only needs a word to shine a light into the darkness.

A sense of humour

I've always been one who enjoys a good laugh. Before I was a pastor the banter and camaraderie of working in a team was great fun. Even when things went wrong you could joke about it with others. I remember one occasion when I had done something wrong and was getting a good telling off from my boss, and he asked me, 'Why didn't you do what you had been told?' My reply was, 'Sheer incompetence on my part.' He thought that answer was hilarious and it took all the sting out of our conversation and we moved on. I must admit that while I've been writing parts of this book, I've had a good chuckle to myself about some of the things that went on 'in the name of God'.

The trouble with pastoring a small church is that there is no team to work with on a daily basis, and so no team camaraderie. There is not much opportunity to have a 'good laugh' about the problems you are facing, and everything can become a little too serious in a gloomy kind of way. I'm not talking about levity or shallowness, but a sense of togetherness with those who are in the same boat. Laughing helps to relieve stress and to put things in the right perspective.

It also didn't help because we had a couple of outspoken members who thought laughing in church (or even smiling) was wrong. More than once I was told that Jesus was a man of sorrows and that there was no Biblical reference to his laughing, only weeping. I tried to reason that Jesus was a man of sorrows so that we could become men and women of joy. The two shortest verses in the Bible prove that wonderfully: 'Jesus wept' (John 11:35) and 'Be joyful always' (1 Thessalonians 5:16). Jesus wept so we could be joyful always, even in church.

I also cannot believe that Jesus went through the whole of his life and ministry without laughing. It is not human not to laugh. (We also have to be very careful in forming a doctrine from the Bible's silence on a matter.) Unfortunately all that I said was of no avail. So if I said anything from the pulpit that raised a smile it was frowned on and criticised by a few. At times this caused me to repress my own natural cheerful character and to feel as though I was in a spiritual straightjacket. Actually one of the members who outlawed laughing in church often went on about how we should 'rejoice with trembling', an excellent quote from Psalm 2. The *funny thing* was I never saw this individual either trembling or rejoicing, so it made a mockery of the point he was trying to make.

I believe we should be serious but not solemn in church. We should rejoice and praise God with all our might. Remember, 'a happy heart makes the face cheerful' (Proverbs 15:13). And as the Shorter Catechism says, we are 'to enjoy him for ever'.

Let me mention one incident that is quite funny on the one hand, but actually turned into a pastoral issue. We had a lady come to church from a rough background. She was in her late sixties, quite poorly in health and not at all used to church ways. She came faithfully every Sunday morning and we were sure the Lord was working in her life, but because of some of the things she did and said, we were never certain that she was born again.

The amusing problem arose because she had a habit of crunching on hard mints during the morning service. As soon as she had finished crunching on one mint, she popped another one into her mouth. Fortunately I could not hear the noise from the pulpit, but for those within range her crunching

Chapter 5

became a real annoyance. So much so that a member of the congregation approached me and strongly exhorted me to have a 'word' with her. Why he could not have spoken to her himself I'm not sure, but I was asked to intervene.

I was conscious that I did not want to upset her, especially as the Lord was speaking to her. So I passed the buck! My wife was on good terms with her and so I asked her to have a quiet chat to see if we could solve 'the problem'. The lady graciously heard what my wife said, understood the issue, and started to suck and chew soft mints instead. Problem solved, or so I thought. After about four weeks she returned to the hard mints and the crunching throughout the service resumed. For some of the members it became such an issue that they refused to sit anywhere near her. One man even threatened to leave the church as a result.

This lady had a non-Christian 'boyfriend' who lived abroad but sometimes came to visit and to stay with her. He had been a hotelier and had self-published a book about his experiences. In one of the chapters he went into great detail about how one of the guests procured a prostitute to keep him company during his stay. What I didn't realise and only discovered after I had retired was that this book was handed out to all the members of the church to read! I just hope they didn't think it came with my recommendation!

Lessons

- Is the pastor allowed to say anything in a church service that makes the congregation smile or laugh? Is he allowed to crack the odd joke? Should he always be a 'man of sorrows' like our Lord? You may think the answer to these questions is obvious. But, believe me, it all depends on who you have in your congregations.

- When we think about the omnipresence and omniscience of the Lord, is there really much difference between a sense of humour in a church service and a sense of humour at home? If our laughter and fun are clean and wholesome, I cannot see the Lord disapproving.

- Don't let a few people with their morose ideas ruin it for everyone else. Yes, the vocal minority can be difficult, but we don't want the church to turn into a glum environment. Are we likely to attract outsiders when they look at our cheerless faces and say, 'I've got enough trouble of my own without joining this church!'

- Some non-Christians look so unhappy and hard with all that life has thrown at them. Surely it would help stimulate their interest in Christianity if we were a happy people. And where better to express corporate joy than in church.

- William Osier said that 'laughter is the music of life'. Someone else said, 'A cheerful countenance has a lot of face value.'

- Scientists are clear that laughter has many beneficial effects. It is indeed 'strong medicine'. Apparently it 'draws people together in ways that trigger healthy physical and emotional changes in the body. It strengthens your immune system, boosts mood, diminishes pain, and protects from the damaging effects of stress. Nothing works faster or more dependably to bring your mind and body back into balance than a good laugh. Humour lightens your burdens, inspires hope, connects you to others, and keeps you grounded, focused and alert. It also helps you release anger and forgive sooner.' Maybe there are so many problems in churches these days because Christians don't laugh enough!

- I saw a couple of signs on the wall of a café not long ago. The first one said: 'A good laugh recharges your battery.' The second one read: 'Don't take life too seriously. Nobody gets out alive anyway.'

Chapter 5

- Let me share two quotes from one of the greatest preachers of all time, Charles Spurgeon: 'I would rather hear people laugh than I would see them asleep in the house of God' and 'I do believe in my heart that there may be as much holiness in a laugh as in a cry.'

- I'm afraid I cannot resist quoting one of Spurgeon's funny comments: Every week, Spurgeon rode to his church in a carriage pulled by two horses, 'Browny' and 'Brandy'. On one occasion, a man came to Spurgeon's house and accused his horses of breaking the Sabbath. Spurgeon replied, 'My horses are Jewish and worship on Saturdays, not Sundays.' Maybe if we responded to criticism with a little more humour it might help everyone.

- Be careful what you say to new people who start attending your church, especially if they are not Christians. If their habits are annoying, like crunching on mints, surely we can show a little grace to put up with the noise.

- Sometimes mature church members need to be told to sort out their own problems, rather than expecting the pastor to do all their 'dirty work'. Coming from the pastor 'a word' might sound too official, too threatening, rather than a friendly chat from a fellow churchgoer.

- It's impossible to know everything that goes on in your church. We just have to trust in the Lord that he knows and is able to deal with all the secret goings on.

Alone but not lonely

One of the major hurdles you have to jump over as the pastor of a small church is to learn to do most of your work alone. You are the only paid employee and have no colleagues. If you are someone who needs the buzz and banter of an office environment or a job where people are coming and going all the time, then pastoring a small church is not for you. Most of your day is spent alone. You pray on your own. You read and study on your own. You prepare sermons on your own. Those three activities take you to about 75% of your week. The opportunity for vibrant fellowship and 'fun' with others is limited. When you visit, it is not for your own benefit, but to help those who might be struggling in one way or another. You probably spend 15% of each week (maybe more) listening to the 'woes' of others.

I was never lonely, but at times I felt alone. The other leaders were busy with their own lives. My only elder lived a long way from the church and so it was not feasible just to pop round for a quick coffee. It was also difficult to make close friends within the church for fear of being accused of favouritism. Getting together with other pastors was possible, but not always convenient and certainly not on a weekly basis.

How wonderful it is to know that the Lord is with us 24 hours a day. But we also need human company if we are to work most effectively. How this is achieved is difficult, especially if you have many responsibilities that you must fulfil each day. The tendency when you are alone is to magnify the difficulties. As they say, a problem shared is a problem halved, but when there is no one around to share the many problems that arise it is easy to become downhearted. Of course you can share things with your wife, but she might be out working or looking after the children or carrying out her own responsibilities.

Temptations can be harder to resist when you are alone. Despondency was one that frequently tripped me up. Just having no one around to chat to about how the Sunday went or how a members' meeting was conducted caused me to look inwards. I became too introspective for my own good. Yes, after-thoughts are necessary and self-examination important, but we must be careful that they do not lead to a morbid soul searching.

Chapter 5

Lessons

- While it is true to say that I never really felt lonely, many pastors do and it is one of the reasons why so many give up. At the time of writing research shows that 40% of pastors have considered leaving the ministry in the last three months. Over 70% of pastors experience loneliness and have no close friends they can trust with personal matters. 'In 1989 a hundred different occupations were surveyed and rated in terms of loneliness, and the second loneliest job on the list was that of minister of the Word' (Joel Beeke and Terry Slachter, *Encouragement for Today's Pastors*, p. 6). These are alarming statistics and underline the importance of true friendship.

- Even great men experience loneliness. In a discussion Martyn Lloyd-Jones was having with other ministers, one of the men commented on the loneliness of the work of the ministry. Lloyd-Jones responded with feeling, to the surprise of those present, 'You speak of loneliness! I am the loneliest man in this room' (Iain Murray, *The Fight of Faith*, p. 461).

- It is essential to have regular contact with other pastors and friends with whom you can be open and honest. Force yourself to make time. Don't just wait for things to happen, because they probably won't. Be proactive and make appointments on a regular basis. The chances are the other pastors you contact are also crying out for fellowship.

- Be honest. Be absolutely honest with a small group of fellow pastors you can trust. Don't pretend your ministry is more successful than it is and don't minimise your personal problems. Say it as it is, with full confidence in God for the future. And remember, your openness will encourage the other men in your group to be equally open. Then you can begin to help each other.

- Sometimes we feel alone because of the issue of confidentiality. Someone shares something with us and then as they are about to leave they say, 'Oh you will keep this confidential, won't you?' I think it is important to have a clear view on confidentiality and then share that with your congregation. For instance, you might think it's right to share everything with your wife or with your elder or both. Well, the congregation need to know that. Sometimes a 'confidential comment' from a member can be an excuse for them to have a go at someone else without any comeback. It is also very difficult to challenge or investigate a 'confidentiality'.

- Try to keep everything in perspective. It is easy to over-analyse a situation or a comment someone has made, and without outside advice from a friend you can come to the wrong conclusions.

- When choosing elders, consider picking men who are about your own age, not too much older or younger. That will hopefully mean you will have more in common with them. Invite them over for a meal, along with their wives, so a genuine friendship can develop.

- Whatever you do, do it to the best of your ability and then leave it with God for him to accomplish his purposes.

When God seems to be absent

This kind of experience is, of course, common to all Christians. Listen to David in Psalm 13: 'How long, O Lord? Will you forget me forever? How long will you hide your face from me?' (Psalm 13:1). And David was described as a man after God's own heart. There are times when darkness seems to surround us and God feels a million miles away. There were times when I felt despondent and poured out my heart to God and yet he did not seem to hear me. When this goes on from one week to the next with little let up, it can be hard to keep your joy in the Lord. This in

Chapter 5

turn affects the congregation, who sense you are not yourself, and their disappointment or discouragement can sometimes lead to criticism. And so a downward spiral begins which can be hard to stop.

Now this might sound unspiritual and it's the kind of thing some evangelicals will criticise, but there were two secular sayings that often helped me. The first was from a Bob Marley song. The words of the song simply say, 'Don't worry, be happy.' In many ways this can be interpreted as good Christian advice (yes, I know Marley was a Rastafarian). Doesn't Jesus tell us not to worry? And Paul counsels us to rejoice in the Lord always. 'Don't worry, be happy' is not a bad philosophy for life and that little saying often helped me to put things into perspective.

The second saying is the last line of the American civil war film *Gone With The Wind*. Rhett Butler (Clark Gable) has just walked out on Scarlett O'Hara (Vivien Leigh) and she is distraught. She flings herself on the stairs, vows to get him back and in a typically dramatic fashion cries, 'After all, tomorrow is another day.' These words helped me on many occasions. If today has gone badly and you are in the dark clouds, just remember that tomorrow is another day. You may have wept today, but tomorrow might bring rejoicing.

There have also been many Scriptures that have encouraged me along the way. I used to type them out and put them on the back of my study door to remind me. Let me share a couple with you. The first comes after Joseph is raised to second in command of all Egypt and, when naming his second son Ephraim, he says 'It is because God has made me fruitful in the land of my suffering' (Genesis 41:52). I took great comfort from that verse. God does not waste our sufferings, but he is able to bring life out of death and turn a curse into a blessing.

Another encouraging verse is found in 1 Kings 8:12. The context is during the time of Solomon when the ark was brought into the temple and the cloud of the glory of the Lord filled the temple to such a degree that the priests could not perform their service. Solomon then said, 'The LORD has said that he would dwell in a dark cloud.' Sometimes I felt as though

I was in a dark cloud and God gave me the promise that he would dwell with me even there. While I appreciate this is not a strict interpretation of the verse, nevertheless that meaning was certainly a real blessing to me personally. These verses gave me the assurance that God had not left me alone in my darkness and pain.

Lessons

- The Puritans often used to talk about 'God's withdrawings', those times when God removes his sensible presence and we feel alone. The key word here is 'sensible'. God never removes his presence from us, but he sometimes withdraws our sense of it.

- We must stand on God's Word at all times. Our feelings can lie to us, trick us and lead us to think unbiblically. Rather, we need to trust what God's Word says and to stand on his promises. We know he will never leave or forsake us, and even when it 'feels' different Biblical truth is what we must depend on. See Romans 8:38–39.

- The sun is always shining behind the clouds. So God's love is always shining down on us even in the midst of a storm. I like what Corrie Ten Boom says: 'When a train goes through a tunnel and it gets dark, you don't throw away the ticket and jump off. You sit still and trust the engineer.'

- Some jewellers put diamonds on a black cloth so they shine more brightly. Sometimes the darkness of God's absence makes our Christian light shine more brightly.

- It is during times of trial that our faith is stretched and strengthened. Just like when the wind blows, an oak tree digs its roots further into the ground thus making it stronger. So when the winds of adversity blow, we place our faith more firmly into Christ. 'Consider it pure joy, my brothers, whenever you face trials of many kinds, because you know that the testing of your faith develops perseverance. Perseverance must finish its work so that you may be mature and complete, not lacking anything' (James 1:2–4). I like what the archbishop of Glasgow Robert Leighton says: 'Adversity is the diamond dust heaven polishes its jewels with.'

- Whenever we hammer a nail we drive it more firmly into the wood. When we are hammered by trials, they hammer us more deeply into Christ.

- It is said of a palm tree that the greater the weight that is hung on its branches, the more it grows and flourishes, which is probably why the church is compared to a palm tree in Song of Songs 7:7.

- Remember when we feel alone that it is not an unusual experience for a Christian. In fact, it is extremely common. And while it should cause us to think about the possible reasons why God has withdrawn his presence, it should not make us fret unduly.

6. What's the response?

I've entitled this section 'What's the response?' because it's important to have in your own mind how you are going to respond to certain situations before they arise. Sometimes these situations happen without warning and can catch you unawares, but if you have already thought carefully about your response, it will help you to deal with them effectively. To be forewarned is to be forearmed.

Church discipline

It is actually hard to exercise Biblical church discipline. The reason being is that in my experience anyone who is reprimanded for doing something sinful, just packs their bags and moves to another church. The new church rarely asks for any kind of reference or recommendation, being only too pleased that someone new wants to join their ranks and boost their numbers. One example that springs to mind is of a lady who had been saying some dreadful things in the church, sowing division left, right and centre. After a conversation I had with her, she wrote me rather an abusive letter and promptly left the church. Within a couple of months she had become a member of another local church. She also joined a para-church organisation with no questions asked. I have recently heard that she has left that organisation for an extremely petty reason.

I remember one pastor friend telling me about a young unmarried couple in his church who were living together. When he confronted them about their behaviour, their response was to say, 'Get real. Everyone is doing it.' They then resigned their membership and went to another church. I had one young man who occasionally came to the church. He professed to be a Christian. One Sunday morning he openly told me that he often witnessed to different women while in bed with them, before or after having sex with them. I was obviously shocked by his admission and

Chapter 6

told him that such behaviour was not acceptable and he needed to repent. I don't think he ever returned to the church.

So it is extremely difficult to exercise effective church discipline without causing further division, and what you do or say needs great wisdom.

Lessons

- It's always tricky to know how to respond when someone talks a good talk, but lives a bad life, when someone preaches 'love thy neighbour' but there is little evidence of love in their own heart. Or when someone only shows love to a few favourite members and is critical of the rest. We need the grace, wisdom and firmness of Jesus to deal with hypocrisy. If we deal with it in the wrong way or with a harsh spirit, it might create mayhem in the church. Richard Baxter says: 'Prudence must be exercised in the proceeding, lest we do more hurt than good … we should deal humbly even when we deal sharply.'

- Whenever you try to exercise church discipline, it is important that the whole leadership are in agreement with the course of action you as the pastor are planning to take. If possible, they should be present when you confront bad behaviour, so that you are not open to false accusations.

- Remember that the purpose of discipline is repentance and restoration, not division and bitterness.

- If someone wants to join your church, try to find out the reasons why they left their previous church. Asking the old pastor may well throw light on the situation. I've found a truer picture is painted when you have a face to face conversation (or telephone conversation) with the old pastor rather than receiving from him a written statement. Not many pastors want to put in writing what they really feel about an individual. So have some specific questions ready for your conversation.

Interestingly, throughout my whole pastorate, only one other pastor actually called me to chat through why someone had left my church.

- You can never stop someone from leaving if they are determined to go. It may actually be one of those 'blessed subtractions'. It is better to have a smaller but harmonious congregation, than an individual causing havoc among the membership. As I write, I have a pastor friend who is being driven to despair and serious health issues by one member of his congregation who is causing so many difficulties. All he wants is for her to leave.

- It is really sad how much trouble just one discontented individual can cause. In some cases they can be instruments of the devil and need to be recognised and resisted as such.

- I wrote a rather tactless letter of rebuke to a member once, citing Proverbs 27:5: 'Better is open rebuke than hidden love' as the reason for doing so. He actually received my letter extremely graciously and with a large dose of humility. And we are still friends! However, looking back, I don't think the letter was really necessary. Perhaps a friendly chat would have been more appropriate. So make sure you think the rebuke is fully warranted before you take the risk (and it is a risk) of trying to exercise church discipline.

- The Baptist minister Alexander MacLaren once said, 'Kindness makes a person attractive. If you would win the world, melt it, do not hammer it.' This excellent advice should also be applied to how we exercise church discipline. The reason we are pastors is not to show others that we are the boss!

- If you have nurtured a relationship of love and respect between yourself and your members, it makes approaching them about a sensitive subject

Chapter 6

easier and your conversation with them is much more likely to be productive.

- Leave room for God to discipline his children according to his good pleasure. Sometimes we can 'jump the gun' in our eagerness to do what is right, without leaving space for God to act. At times our best way forward is just to keep quiet and pray. A regular reading of Hebrews 12:5–13 is a must when it comes to discipline.

Numbers

Numbers in a small church are vitally important. There is great rejoicing when someone new comes along and it can be heartbreaking when a solid and faithful member leaves, especially if the whole family go too. In a big church the comings and goings are often not really noticed. But in a small church a departure can leave a gaping hole that can take years to fill.

I would imagine that every pastor of a small church wants his congregation to grow not just spiritually but numerically. Perhaps before I go on I should quote from John Benton's helpful book *The Big Picture for Small Churches*. He says that the rule of thumb from an organisation that produces a lot of statistics goes something like this, 'Churches with a usual attendance of over 300 people were looked upon as very large. More than 150 people put the church in the "large" bracket. Over 50 or 60 people meant you belonged to the "average" category. But less than 50 or 60 people meant that they looked upon the church as small' (p. 10). So when I'm talking about numbers I am really referring to 'small' churches.

In small churches the congregation is often made up of older people. That means that the first battle you have as far as numbers are concerned is to get more people into the church than the number you bury. In my first six months of the pastorate I buried six members. That meant I had to find one new member a month just to break even numbers wise.

I must admit I became a little obsessed with numbers. I never counted the congregation as I know some churches do, but I could easily tell if our numbers were going up or down. For the first couple of years as the numbers increased quite quickly everyone was happy. We looked forward to an encouraging future. We even crept into the 'average' category, reaching about 70 in the morning at one point if we included non-members. Considering we started with about 25, this was a sign of blessing on the church, so I concluded. But then for the next few years things tailed off, and one or two comments were made such as, 'Why have new people stopped coming?' One lady even told me the Lord was no longer blessing the church because no one new was coming. All this notches up the pressure on the pastor to get more people in. If we are not careful, we fall into the trap of what I call 'jumboism'.

After that levelling-off period our numbers started to go down. Some were legitimate departures, others just left without any explanation. Five or six left because they were unhappy. A few more died, and a lovely couple decided to return to their family in Scotland. But we weren't getting replacements and so the numbers dropped to about 45 in the morning and about 35 in the evening. We were 'small' again. People started to get discouraged. Some searched for a reason. 'Who can we blame?' I didn't have the answers as to why this was happening. I, too, felt the discouragement, although I kept telling myself, 'It's not about numbers.'

One thing I noticed, though, was that whenever I went to another church (preaching), or to a conference, fraternal—wherever I went—I was asked the same questions: 'How many do you get going to your church? Is it growing (meaning in numbers)?' Some pastors took great delight in telling me about their 'success stories' and the mini-revival that was taking place in their church, which they insinuated was partly down to their preaching skills (which of course may have been true). There was great pressure put on me unwittingly by well-meaning colleagues and inquirers, and that pressure was all to do with numbers. Of course, when we were growing it was great to be able to pass that on, but I was not so keen to shout from the rooftops that our numbers were going down.

Chapter 6

I also found when I went to conferences that the speakers, who were often men who had seen real growth in numbers in their churches, often pushed for small churches to make major modernisations, to bring in the new and dispense with the old, with the view of attracting a younger generation and so boosting the numbers. I remember leaving several conferences thinking, 'How on earth am I going to do what they suggest without destroying the church?' It was even proposed on more than one occasion that I should close my church, leave it a couple of months, then reopen with a new, fresh and exciting congregation. I had visions of reopening without the old congregation and without a new one to replace it! I think I was unduly influenced by all this 'modernisation' talk. I did not take into consideration, as fully as I should have done, my own congregation and their particular needs when I tried to implement small changes.

Lessons

- You have probably heard many times the statement, 'It is not all about numbers', and yet so much of what we are taught and read suggest it *is* all about numbers. When our numbers are increasing we are told that God is pouring out his blessing. When our numbers decrease, God is withholding his blessing. This kind of talk can give both false encouragement when numbers are rising, and false discouragement when numbers are falling.

- We must have it burned into our souls that God does not despise the day of small things. Other people may do. The world certainly does. But God does not. As long as we are serving God to the best of our ability, we must leave 'numbers' and results up to him. I am not a good example to follow in this regard. Listen to what Jesus said about the teachers of the law and Pharisees: 'You must obey them and do everything they tell you. But do not do what they do, for they do not practise what they preach.' So do everything I tell you in this regard, but don't do as I did!

- The doctrine of the remnant was a great help to me, with examples such as Gideon's three hundred-strong army and Israel being one of the smallest nations (Deuteronomy 7:7). Only eight were saved from the flood and Lot and his family alone escaped from Sodom. Jesus chose just twelve disciples and not twelve hundred. God has a completely different mind-set to many in the church when it comes to numbers.

- There is no need to castigate yourself over numbers. Yes, if you feel there is a specific reason why the congregation is shrinking, then that needs to be addressed. But to become overly self-critical just because someone leaves who does not 'appreciate your preaching' or your 'style of leadership' is unnecessary.

- Try not to become disheartened if a lovely Christian family start coming for a couple of months and you have great hopes that they might join you, then they disappear, never to be seen or heard of again. I always found that disappointment hard to take. I should have been more philosophical and trusted more fully in the purposes of God.

- I remember one delightful couple who came to the church, and I was hopeful they would join us and be a great blessing. Sadly they left after a while. When I managed to chat with them sometime afterwards, they told me they had not stayed because of someone in my congregation (a non-member) who had caused considerable trouble in their previous church. This was particularly discouraging as I would have willingly swapped them for the troublemaker!

- Speak to the congregation about what's going on in the church and try to allay any fears about the numbers falling. Often a little word here or there can lift the morale. Nor do I think it is wrong to mention the reasons why people have left. It might quash numerous rumours. I

Chapter 6

always struggled when members left 'secretly' and would never disclose, even when asked, why they had decided to move on.

- Beware of pride. Could it be we want a larger congregation because of what people might think? We can boast more loudly. We will receive more praise from others. We will be regarded as 'successful' by many. 'Pride goes before destruction, a haughty spirit before a fall' (Proverbs 16:18).

- While I'm sure we would love a larger congregation and it can be a sign of blessing, there are other ways to measure growth. Growth in love for Christ, in knowledge, in sacrifice, in joy and so on. Don't be blinkered to just one way. And remember, just because something works, it does not mean it is right. As Martyn Lloyd-Jones said, 'Popularity and numbers are a very false test of truth.'

- In the end our dependency is on God to do as he pleases, not on our efforts or expertise. 'Trust in the Lord with all your heart and lean not on your own understanding; in all your ways acknowledge him, and he will direct your paths' (Proverbs 3:5–6).

When people leave

Although I have talked a little about people leaving, I think this topic deserves a separate section. My church was in an area of the country where there were many different churches to choose from and it was quite common for people to 'church hop', or to act like 'spiritual gypsies', going to a different church most Sundays. It is also true that in bigger churches only a small proportion of the congregation know the reason why someone has left their congregation, whereas in my small church quite a few seemed to know, or at least tried to find out, and everyone had an opinion on the rights and wrongs of their move.

What's the response?

I was speaking to a pastor of a small church just recently who told me that a family had left his church and gone to my old church. When I asked the reason why, he said it was because, according to the family, he was 'in error' in the way he was leading the church and for that reason they could not stay. When I inquired further what that meant, expecting some great heresy, it turned out that because repentance and faith were not mentioned in every sermon, that constituted the 'error'. The family had left without any warning, leaving hurt and a big hole in the church.

One thing I noticed was that I was often blamed by some for those who left the church during my pastorate, but I was never given credit for those who came. Many more came than left, but that didn't seem to matter. One man, completely out of the blue, told me on several occasions that I was the reason some people had left. Now that may have been true but why he had to keep on telling me I'm not sure. On one Sunday he even stayed behind after everyone had gone home to tell me.

There is no doubt that I was upset when someone left and I took it personally. Sometimes it was a bit of a personality clash, sometimes they didn't agree with something that was going on in the church, sometimes it was for legitimate reasons, such as moving away. But I always felt disappointed.

Lessons

- You will be amazed at some of the reasons people leave a church. Maybe they don't like the way you gesticulate when you are preaching, or the colour of your tie, or how the flowers are arranged. Perhaps the change you made to the order of service is disliked. One lady left because 'she felt it was the right time', whatever that means! Speaking of ties reminds me of an occasion I was preaching at another church (wearing a tie) and after the service a man came up to me and flicked my tie and said an earnest 'thank you'. It turned out he was more grateful for my tie than my sermon! I found out that in that particular church

Chapter 6

there was 'controversy' about whether or not the preacher should wear a tie.

- From my experience there are all sorts of reasons people give for leaving a church: I have been offended, I don't like the music, the pastor shouts too much (one lady stopped attending because when I got passionate in preaching and raised my voice she thought I was angry), my friends have left, the preaching isn't 'sound' enough, I don't like the pastor. We could go on and on! It would be a useful exercise to take a few minutes to write down all the *Biblical* reasons for leaving a church and for joining another one.

- Try not to be too harsh on yourself when someone leaves. It can be really discouraging, but keep your eyes on Jesus and trust him. As you are the leader and call the shots, the reason why someone leaves is probably going to be something to do with what you have done or said. Try to be philosophical about it, while learning from any mistakes.

- You can't please all of the people all of the time.

- Sometimes it's good to offer a member a sincere apology if you feel their criticism is just. We all make mistakes. Own up and repent and where necessary seek reconciliation.

- It may be a member is unwilling to tell you why he or she is about to leave. I wouldn't go out of your way to find the reason. Respect their decision to remain silent and pray for them that the Lord will guide and use them in the future.

- Should you chase after a member who unexpectedly leaves the church? Well, it depends on the individual and the circumstances, but it would certainly be worth having a conversation with them in case the situation can be resolved. However, if they have been causing problems, you must ask yourself the question: 'Do I really want them to stay?' Perhaps I shouldn't admit this, but there were several resignations that I thanked God for!

- Never forget the sovereignty of God. It is his church and he will accomplish his purposes despite the weaknesses of the pastor and the fickleness of the congregation.

7. Afterword

I think it is important to try to answer the question: 'How has the pastorate changed me?' It is true that I have experienced some dark times since I left, times of despair, feelings of uselessness and doubts over my leadership qualities. Sometimes I have been too harsh on myself, taking one hundred percent of the blame for everything negative that happened and concluding that my ministry was a failure. Occasionally I have wondered if I left the church too soon. Could I have come through the difficulties, sorted out the problems and survived to tell the tale? Hindsight is a wonderful thing but not much good when you have already left. What is clear is the faithfulness of God towards me during my retirement years. It has not been easy 'recovering' from my experience, but God is gently and slowly rebuilding what was a rather shattered life.

There is no doubt that one of the negative effects of the problems I went through has been to make me less trusting and more cynical of people and the things they say and do. Because there were some Christians who could change 'colour' like a chameleon, from a glorious white in public to a devilish black in private, it has made me more suspicious of people's motives and actions. One lady in the congregation appeared all sweetness and light on a Sunday, smiling nicely at me, but during the week she was going around people's houses falsely accusing me of all sorts of things in an attempt to stir others up against me. When I first discovered what was happening I could hardly believe it because of her Sunday charade!

A suspicious nature is not a good trait to have and usually springs from resentments that we hold. While we have to be as wise as serpents and not anyone's fool, the Bible tells us that 'love always trusts' (1 Corinthians 13:7). Forgiveness is vital for a healthy Christian and there is no legitimate reason we can present to God for holding on to bitterness. The Bible exhorts us to make sure 'no one misses the grace of God and that no bitter root grows up to cause trouble and defile many' (Hebrews 12:15). This is an area that many former pastors, including myself, struggle to obtain the victory.

As mentioned above, unforgiveness has been a real issue with me. After I had left the pastorate I kept going over the same ground and presenting to myself a host of reasons why I should not forgive. Of course none of them were Biblical and none pleasing or acceptable to God, but it was an area that defeated me on many occasions. I knew what I was feeling was wrong, that it was only hurting my own walk with God, and that there needed to be a deep repentance and change in my heart, but at the time these thoughts did not help. It was only the goodness and grace of God over time that softened me and enabled me to move on, although I must admit I still have the occasional bad day.

Conversely to the above, I have become more sympathetic to those who are struggling or in pain or being tempted in various ways. I 'feel' more, to such an extent that when I hear a sad story I have to hold back the tears more than I have ever done. I'm not the 'crying' type, but I now empathise more deeply and easily and I am less indifferent towards the hurts and tribulations many face. Just recently a pastor I know told me how a group are trying to drive him out of the church he has led for many years. He only has two years to go before he retires. He has withdrawn from the situation 'to let them get on with it'. All the stress he has experienced has brought on signs of early dementia, so he won't be able to return even if the congregation has a change of heart. After many decades of faithful ministry this is a terribly sad way to end. My heart goes out to him.

My own 'hurtful' experiences have changed my preaching for the better, I hope. I have become a 'softer' preacher, not so harsh or judgemental. I now want to preach on verses like 'A bruised reed he will not break and a smouldering wick he will not snuff out' (Isaiah 42:3). At the beginning of my ministry I was more inclined to preach from passages such as Zephaniah 1:14–18. Now I want my preaching to help, restore and heal as I realise how many ordinary people in any congregation are hurting. I have just finished a sermon on how to cope with depression, from Psalm 13. So the Lord has changed my focus from the 'wrath of God' to the hope we have in Jesus.

I am less rigid in some areas of doctrine. This does not mean I have compromised one iota on the essential doctrines of the Christian faith, but I am less rigid on those doctrines where true Christians hold different views. I no longer think, 'I'm right and everyone else is wrong.' I can understand differences more easily and I have a greater appreciation of the opinions others hold. I'm less likely to argue my point of view in an aggressive tone. The intenseness with which I used to hold certain doctrines has mellowed. For instance, I hold an a-millennial position regarding the end times. Today I will no longer ex-communicate you if you are a pre- or post-millennial!

I am more tolerant of different styles of worship. I used to be quite critical if the services were not conducted in the way I thought best. I now appreciate that worship does not always have to be conducted in the old Puritanical style for God to honour it. I realise with more grace that some like to sing the old hymns and some prefer the new. Some like the music loud and fast, others slow and soft. It is not necessarily right to say one way is better than the other. I am more appreciative of a Charismatic style of worship, where I see great joy and a love for Christ. I am less attracted to an old fashioned type of service, which can be rigid and inflexible. Surely it is possible to modernise our worship while keeping it reverent and Christ-centred. Although I will add that if a congregation do not want to change their style of worship it is almost impossible for the pastor to initiate that change without stirring up a mountain of trouble.

I have learned in a more practical way that all things are under God's sovereign control, even those times of suffering and unhappiness. God uses pain for our good and changes our character through it. Nothing is wasted with him and all things work for the good. He is our Father, who loves us. I have sometimes asked myself, 'Did I quit the pastorate too soon?' But when I focus on the sovereignty of God and remember the reality of what

Afterword

I was experiencing, I think I made the right decision at the right time. Yes, I have regrets and look back with a measure of disappointment that things did not work out for the better, but I have learned to cast them at the feet of Jesus and trust him.

The final question I must ask is: 'Would I go back into the pastorate?' I doubt it, partly because of my age and partly because 'once bitten, twice shy', although with the Lord we should never say never! I certainly would not go back into running a small church on my own as the permanent pastor. I might be willing to help for a set period of time while the congregation look for a new man, but I would not consider being that new man. If a position in a larger church came knocking, with the opportunity to work in a team, I would consider it, but it would have to be extremely appealing.

While it is true to say that there are times when I wish I had never become a pastor in the first place, because of the scars I still bear, I know that my Father led me by the hand into that responsibility and I thank him for the opportunity to serve him in such a way.